Tidings of Troubled Times

Tidings of Troubled Times

MANISH TEWARI

PALIMPSEST

Published by Palimpsest Publishers 2017
Palimpsest Publishing House Pvt. Ltd.
16 Community Centre, Panchsheel Park
New Delhi 110017, India

ISBN 978 – 93 – 82622 – 23 – 9

Typeset in Stone Serif by Punyabrata Pattrea
Printed and bound in India by Thomson Press India Ltd.

To the Last Liberals
of the World
Still Standing.... !

CONTENTS

PART I

INDO-PAK RELATIONS: THE CONFLICT-PEACE SYNDROME

CHINESE CHEQUERS

THE WORLD IN A FLUX

US IN A POST-HEGEMONIC WORLD

PART II

THE INSTITUTIONAL CHALLENGE

...Why?

At Yad Vashem, Israel's official memorial to the Holocaust victims in Jerusalem a quote from a German Pastor, Martin Niemöller, summed up the Nazi monstrosity rather poignantly:

First they came for the Socialists, and I did not speak out–
Because I was not a Socialist.

Then they came for the Trade Unionists, and I did not speak out–
Because I was not a Trade Unionist.

Then they came for the Jews, and I did not speak out–
Because I was not a Jew.

Then they came for me – and there was no one left to speak for me.

As I absorbed those prophetic words another impassioned plea flashed through my mind. The great English poet and political activist, John Milton, author of Paradise Lost, appealed to the Parliament of England for the liberty of speech. This 1644 argument in scintillating prose is known as Areopagitica. If you read it even now, the ringing words electrify your being: 'Give me the liberty to know, to utter, and to argue freely according to conscience, above all liberties.' For when silence is mistaken for acquiescence it becomes a crime to stay silent. As Mohandas Karamchand Gandhi put it rather succinctly, 'silence becomes cowardice when occasion demands speaking out the whole truth and acting accordingly.'

At a point in time when freedom of speech and expression guaranteed in the Constitution as a fundamental right is coming under sustained assault in India where any criticism of the government is being dubbed as anti-national, questioning the establishment is equivalent to treason, and even intra-institution dialogue is being muffled, this collection of articles written over the past year or so mostly for various newspapers, would have remained scattered and perhaps even sucked into the black hole of time but for the efforts of friends at Palimpsest. They meticulously put them together between the covers of a book. This is my ode to free speech. Let freedom reign...

New Delhi **Manish Tewari**

15 August 2017

Part I

Indo-Pak Relations: The Conflict-Peace Syndrome

BRIDGE PARTITION

There's a popular belief that at the people-to-people level, all is well between India and Pakistan, and the problem is really between the establishments in the two nations. But is that assumption really correct?

A retired Pakistani general narrated a story at a recent Track-2 event on how young officers posted at the border or Line of Control would see visiting civilian friends or relatives exult in excitement if they spotted an Indian soldier on the other side. Invariably, many would pick up a stone and hurl it at the Indian soldier to express 'hate' towards the 'enemy'.

A retired Indian officer recounted the spectre of pulp patriotism that plays itself out regularly at Wagah when the ceremonial lowering of the flag takes place in the evening. Civilians from both sides give full vent to their lung capacity while waving their respective national flags.

A ceremony described by a finance and external affairs minister in the Atal Behari Vajpayee government thus: 'We have that ugly ceremony at Wagah, almost vulgar, I don't know why we are continuing with it, but we are.' This machismo has been going on since 1959.

There's the hysteria over cricket matches between the two countries. The mood in both nations is supercharged as though it wasn't a game but the two countries were at war. Then there's the problem of Pakistani textbooks in which Indians are vilified as cunning and scheming Hindus. Much like Jews were disparaged in the inter-war years and for centuries earlier in many parts of Europe.

The question that often pops up is: Are post-Partition generations in India blasé about Pakistan? The answer, unfortunately, is a big 'no'. While the generation that saw the ravages of Partition on both sides undoubtedly had scars seared into their collective psyche, there were some redeeming features too. In moments of nostalgia, they would also reminisce, perhaps among themselves, about the good times - how they had lived and played together before neighbours turned against neighbours. It perhaps made the trauma liveable.

But the memories they passed on to their children and grandchildren were ghoulish tales of savagery, butchery, pillage, rape, and slaughter. All unfortunately true. The effect this had on impressionable young minds was to crystallize the fear that everything and everybody on the other side was an evil ogre. The passed-on narrative thus got superimposed on an already tragic reality, reinforcing stereotypes in each family's folklore.

Complementing and supplementing this is the legacy of four wars, cross-border terrorism, radicalization, and a host of other negatives. Even in popular perceptions, there is hardly any positive strand in the past six decades that automatically comes to mind.

If there was not such a fertile field of subliminal hate in the hearts and minds of people on both sides, television channels wouldn't have been able to harvest it for TRPs. If one does a sentiment analysis of social-media platforms whenever anything on the India-Pakistan paradigm crops up, all that one hears are expletive-laden posts and vile pictorial depictions. It begs the obvious query: If all is well between the peoples of

India and Pakistan, then why are all these parameters negative? It therefore means that while they may be civil to each other socially, deep down, the animosity runs as strong as the antipathy between the two establishments.

Is there a need to transform this narrative or should we allow the discourse of hate and antipathy run its natural course? South Asia, the world's most populous region, is hostage to this India-Pakistan rivalry, but it is important to ensure that those living on opposite sides of the border or Line of Control see each other as real people in flesh and blood.

There may be many myths about the *pappi-jhappi* (hugs and kisses) revelry between the two peoples, but the fact is that only a minuscule number of India's 1.2 billion population have actually seen or met a Pakistani. The converse is also true. There's an urgent need to humanize them for each other. This can only happen if travel restrictions are eased. The ones that we fear don't apply for visas to cross over – they come with weapons in boats or over mountains. The ones we stop by making the visa-issuing process difficult end up becoming their core constituency. In the absence of an alternative narrative and a chance to size each other up, they become natural fodder for the purveyors of the hate propaganda.

In Europe, after the Second World War, young people could travel the length and breadth of the continent with just one rail pass. This was part of a well-conceived plan to whittle down the legacy of hatred that had consumed millions of lives in Europe.

Can a young person in South Asia with a single ticket backpack across the region? The answer is 'no'. It would not take a rocket scientist to figure out why.

Why can't we have joint concerts with both Indian and Pakistani artistes at Wagah and other border crossings at least twice a year, telecast live across both nations? Surely, if we can have military ceremonies daily, we can have music on two days to demonstrate our shared syncretic cultural heritage. It's strange that while you can read every Pakistani newspaper and see every TV channel on the Internet, they are proscribed in India. The converse is true in Pakistan too, though many Indian channels are available over a DTH platform. While rabid ones should not get downlinking permission, the question is: How successful has the government been in controlling their illegal proliferation.

Similarly, why hasn't any entertainment channel thought about a Masterchef India-Pakistan or South Asia, or a street food face-off taking the region's culinary diversity into the homes of ordinary people? Why is the hunt for young music sensations limited to the territory of a country? Why can't we have a South Asian version of the Eurovision Song Contest?

While these may not lead to any solution of the so-called 'core issues' between the two countries, these are really premised on the classical Westphalian concept of a nation state, a construct based on borders and geographical boundaries between nations, which the Internet and social media are making almost irrelevant with virtual sovereign universes like Facebook Nation and Twitter lands being in play.

What these initiatives might do is perhaps mitigate the latent bitterness we have internalized as a people. It would make the resolution of contested geographical questions more palatable as these would ultimately involve some give and take if they don't become simply redundant. It is important to get the acoustics right and achieve 'real peace' in our times. Not, of course, one that is of the Neville Chamberlain variety!

The Asian Age
24 July 2016

AVOID TRUMPIFICATION OF INDIA-PAK DIALOGUE

India's home minister went for a SAARC conference to Islamabad, where the Pakistanis received him in 'great style', with demonstrations led by the likes of Hizbul Mujahideen chief Syed Salahuddin, and Jama'at-ud-Da'wah boss Hafiz Saeed, who is also the reigning high priest of the proscribed terror outfit Lashkar-e-Taiba. This was perhaps the first time that Pakistan permitted and patronized anti-India rallies in the heart of its capital during a multilateral conference.

Complementing the Pakistani belligerence was the stream of rhetoric emanating from the Indian side, essentially underscoring the fact that there would be no bilateral engagement between India and Pakistan during the Islamabad meeting. It then begs two obvious questions. First, why did the home minister travel to Islamabad? How did things come to such a pass so quickly once again in the undulant India-Pakistan tango?

South Asia is the world's least integrated region, hostage to the zero-sum game between India and Pakistan. This non-relationship between the two also has taken on a nuclear dimension over the past 18 years. If India and Pakistan are again talking at each other rather than trying to talk to each other, reiterating clichéd positions, then the SAARC ministerial meeting itself is a futile exercise.

The only plausible rationale for Rajnath Singh's visit to Islamabad can then possibly be the misplaced machismo that 'I can and have come to rant at you in your country.' This doesn't at all augur well for the region.

In the chequered history of the two nations, there have been innumerable flashpoints. But has the situation been ever so bad in the absence of the high-voltage trigger that is intrinsic to such virtual conflagrations? No.

If one looks back over the past 16 years since the Kargil conflict, there were three high-profile sparks that could have unleashed a disastrous chain of events between the two countries. The hijacking of IC814 from Kathmandu to Kandahar in December 1999, the attack on the Indian Parliament in December 2001 and Operation Parakram launched subsequently by the Indian Army and, of course, the 26/11-terror attack on Mumbai in November 2008. All these outrages bore the indelible stamp of Pakistan's deep state and the ISI's nexus with non-state actors.

But despite the grave and unwarranted provocation that were seen during the terms of Prime Ministers Atal Behari Vajpayee and Manmohan Singh, New Delhi avoided any escalation, much to the frustration of India's inflamed public opinion, as there was an acute realization in the government that there are no quantifiable benchmarks or predictable scenarios to an acceleration of hostilities. At which red line would the nuclear dimension come into play, and in an evolving confrontation, were all red lines and thresholds not subject to continuous reappraisal?

The difference between then and now is that even in the absence of a 'trigger', both India and Pakistan seem hell-bent on a game of dangerous brinkmanship. Of course, there has been a bout of violence in Kashmir that has claimed innocent lives and put the security forces under greater stress, but it isn't the first time it has happened.

It's a cycle that will keep repeating itself till the time the Indian state doesn't look at options beyond the usual security solutions. At some point, and ignoring the jingoism unleashed by certain television channels, the Indian state must take a call on whether it simply wants to hold on to territory in Kashmir, or also keep the people on its side.

The essence of any counter-insurgency doctrine is to win over the hearts and minds of the people; for an insurgency can be isolated and brought to its knees only if it loses the oxygen of local partisan support. In Kashmir, we seem to have elevated alienation to a veritable fine art.

To return, meanwhile, to the India–Pakistan conundrum, why are Narendra Modi and Nawaz Sharif pressing the hate buttons so cynically? Is it because of electoral calculations? In Pakistan's case, it doesn't square up, as in its last national elections India was a non-issue. Also, to a large extent, Pakistan was not on the agenda during the 2014 general election in India.

If the idea is to once again tap into Partition's fault lines to dredge up and tilt at windmills of the two-nation theory, then both establishments are playing with fire. If Mr Modi wants to subliminally play the 'unreliability card' vis-à-vis India's Muslims, it's an extremely myopic and dangerous game of smoke and mirrors, one with grave implications. Mr Modi played this number in the 2002, 2007 and 2012 Gujarat polls with a different cast of characters each time, but with the same divisive message. But it's a very dangerous play risking a prime minister. The Trumpification of politics in the South Asian context is fraught with large pits that can lead to huge falls.

For Mr Sharif to try to ride this tiger is akin to cruising for a bruising. There's a huge constituency of fanatics in Pakistan, far more rabid and venomously anti-India than the Pakistan People's Party and Pakistan Muslim League (Nawaz) could ever be. By starting down that track, that country's mainstream political parties would squarely play into the hands of the fringe; and unlike in India, there are no significant minorities to beat up in Pakistan and generate xenophobia for electoral purposes.

The somersaults, U-turns and flip-flops that characterized New Delhi's approach towards Pakistan in the past 26 months could earlier have been put down to the new bunch in South Block being out of depth, that allowed the Pakistani deep state to run circles around them. However, with each passing day, the desire to push the envelope further and ratchet up tensions in a calibrated way points to a more sinister and ominous game plan aimed at playing the Pakistan card for domestic purposes.

If Mr Modi believes he can sow this wind, he should be under no illusion that the resulting whirlwind would have catastrophic long-term consequences - both domestically and internationally. This is also true for Nawaz Sharif.

The Asian Age
6 August 2016

JINGOISM ON BALOCHISTAN IS NOT IN INDIA'S INTEREST

The prime minister's reference to Pakistan Occuoied Kashmir (PoK), the Shia Muslim-dominated areas of Gilgit and Baltistan and the troubled province of Balochistan in his Independence Day address from the ramparts of the Red Fort was perhaps the most explicit admission that his Pakistan policy or the lack of it lies in absolute tatters.

In the last 26 months, the NDA/BJP government's approach towards Pakistan has swung from the sublime to the ridiculous. It would be worthwhile recapping the trajectory of this non-strategy. In the flush of victory, the prime minister invited the heads of SAARC nations and beyond for his coronation on 26 May 2014. Barely had the invite reached Islamabad than the Indian consulate in Herat, Afghanistan was attacked by the ISI sponsored Lashkar-e-Taiba militants on 23 May, a fact confirmed by none other than the then Afghan President Hamid Karzai. Rather than withdrawing the invite, the Indian Prime Minister designate and his acolytes pulled out every stop to ensure Nawaz Sharif's presence at the crowning of the freshly minted Tsar of South Asia.

Modi's Flawed Pakistan Policy

After a round of *jhappi-pappis* (hugs and kisses) the Modi government decided to try out their brand of muscular diplomacy. Just before the scheduled foreign secretary-level talks in August 2014 in New Delhi, the Indian establishment drew a line in the sand declaring that the Pakistani High Commissioner cannot invite the Hurriyat leadership to tea at his residence during the talks, a practice that every prime minister from Narasimha Rao onwards had wisely ignored.

The cancellation of the talks succeeded by unprecedented firing across the international border and the Line of Control, something not witnessed in the previous ten years.

While the official boycott of Pakistan was still on, Narendra Bhai Damodardas Modi met Nawaz Sharif surreptitiously on the sidelines of the SAARC summit in Kathmandu in November 2014, a meeting allegedly brokered by a steel oligarch. What transpired at the meeting no one knows, but the stalemate continued for another six months.

Suddenly on the sidelines of another multilateral meeting in Ufa in Russia in July 2015, Modi and Nawaz Sharif had a highly visible photo-op and issued a joint statement that they would talk about terror. For the Pakistanis, this was a major coup because for 10 long years, the BJP had kept parroting that terror and talks couldn't go hand-in-hand. In a complete reversal of that position, now they signed a joint proclamation that they would talk about terror.

Once the Pakistanis got what they wanted, they promptly went back on the joint statement and even before the ink had dried, tossed it into the dustbin of history. What followed was an ugly match of cross-border verbal kabbadi between the Indian foreign minister and her Pakistani counterpart Sartaj Aziz. Pakistan supplemented the verbal assault with a terror attack in Gurdaspur in Punjab, a state that had been free from the scourge of terrorism for over two decades since 1995.

Flip-Flops Continue

Another clandestine meeting in Bangkok in November 2015 between India's National Security Advisor Ajit Doval and his newly minted Pakistani counterpart, General Janjua, succeeded the disastrous Ufa summit. No details of this interaction were ever made public, unprecedented in a functional democracy like India.

On 25 December 2015 news broke at noon that Prime Minister Modi had decided to visit Lahore on his way back from Afghanistan. Given the tumultuous relationship between Afghanistan and Pakistan, this was a diplomatic blunder that was strictly avoidable. It is like going to Bejing from Tokyo given the history between the two Asian neighbours, a mistake that Pranab Mukherjee made way back in 2006 as defence minister.

Why did Prime Minister Modi decide to go to Lahore? Was it for confabulations, attending Nawaz Sharif's granddaughter's wedding festivities, or for sampling the fare in Anarkali Bazaar? No one knows. No details were ever made public of what transpired.

The deep state in Pakistan reciprocated the visit by launching another attack, this time at the Pathankot airbase in Punjab. After much hand-wringing by India, in another tactical folly, they permitted a Pakistani investigation team to visit Pathankot to see the evidence that the attackers were Pakistanis. The Pakistani joint investigation team that had officers from the rogue ISI on it, promptly went back and rubbished the Pathankot terror attack as an attempt by the Indians to tar Pakistan with a black brush. The Pakistanis did not allow a reciprocal visit by the Indian investigation agencies to conclusively nail the credentials of the Pakistani terrorists neutralized in the attack.

Being Manipulated by Pakistan

In the midst of all this, the foreign minister travelled to Islamabad for the Heart of Asia Conference, the home minister to Pakistan for the SAARC ministerial meetings but on no substantive issue did the speedometer of dialogue between the two countries move even a millimetre.

What became increasingly clear to the evil ogre called the Pakistani establishment was that they were dealing with a bunch of amateurs in South Block and they could run in circles around them at will.

This frustration at being taken for a ride by the Pakistanis finally found articulation in the prime minister's Independence Day speech. The Pakistani generals and their civilian factotums have been past masters at this game. They have made a monkey out of the Americans and their allies by taking their billions yet sheltering the likes of Osama bin Laden. They have skilfully manipulated the Chinese to the extent of getting them to provide illicit nuclear and missile technology in the 90s and now persuading them to underwrite the cost of developing Pakistan's infrastructure in the form of $46 billion China-Pakistan Economic Corridor (CPEC).

However, it is worth examining as to how tenable the prime minister's jingoism is. Is the dismemberment of Pakistan in India's interest? The answer is no.

Let us presume that Pakistan, riven by its internal contradictions and the centrifugal tendencies at play, disintegrates on its own without even an iota of encouragement from India and a million Muslim refugees land up at Wagah. What will India do, given that the scars of Partition are still deeply etched in the psyche of Indian Punjab?

Stable Pakistan in India's Interest

You do not have to look further than Afghanistan to discern as to what strife in that country has done to Pakistan. Consider for that matter the West's stupidity in trying to re-open the status quo of the Sykes-Picot agreement after the dismemberment of the Ottoman empire and its impact on Europe. Therefore, howsoever unpalatable it may sound and un-pulp-patriotic it may be, it is in India's interest to have a stable, integrated Pakistan.

Given the fact that Prime Minister Modi may not agree with this proposition and may want to play hardball with Pakistan, is the return of Pakistan Occuoied Kashmir, the Northern Areas or Gilgit-Baltistan or even the independence of Balochistan feasible without an internal upsurge in the foreseeable future?

Drawing Parallels between PoK and Balochistan

It is true that both the Northern Areas and the PoK were a part of erstwhile state of Jammu and Kashmir, acceded to India in entirety by Maharaja Hari Singh on 26 October 1947. However, it is equally factual that even in 1947-48, Gilgit was the only part of the erstwhile princely state that was not contested for recapture by the Indian surface forces.

The much-quoted 1994 resolution of the Indian Parliament that the only unfinished business of Partition is the return of the PoK also has a context to it. The US point person for South Asia at that time, Robin Raphel, and by extension her then boss President Bill Clinton, were questioning the accession of J&K to India and giving us much grief at international fora including the United Nations Human Rights Commission. It was in those circumstances that the resolution was adopted. Please remember it was before the 1998 nuclear tests that froze the power balance in South Asia into perpetuity.

Similarly, the tragedy of Balochistan has been a continuing one since 1947 when the erstwhile state of Kalat (much of modern Balochistan) was forcibly annexed by the Pakistani armed forces. The battle for liberation has been raging unremittingly in that province for decades now. The atrocities of the Pakistan Army, their kill and dump squads have been documented not only by Baloch nationalists but by the international community as well.

Modi is not Vajpayee

In 2009, at Sharm el-Sheikh, when a reference to Balochistan albeit at Pakistan's instance, was included in the joint statement that would have given India an opportunity to expose the perfidy of Pakistan, the BJP screamed blue murder alleging that Dr Manmohan Singh had acquiesced to the Pakistani insinuation that India interferes in its internal affairs. The UPA government unfortunately also balked and did not precipitate matters, which the Baloch struggle deserved.

However, in the last two years, did Prime Minister Modi, his NSA or his ministers ever raise this issue with their Pakistani interlocutors? The answer is No. If they were so chary about interference into the internal affairs of other nations, then how does the prime minister's bombast square with that. Is India now going to extend moral, material or tactical support to the Baloch struggle? Have the Afghan and Iranian concerns been factored into this equation?

Drawing parallels between the liberation of Bangladesh and Balochistan is completely asinine. The independence of Bangladesh was a brilliantly executed politico-military strategy by a leadership of a completely different calibre. India, despite the 1962 Chinese debacle and the 1965 stalemate with Pakistan, enjoyed superiority in conventional terms in 1971 and the Mukti Bahini had played its own role too.

Vajpayee was not unpatriotic when he went to Minar-e-Pakistan at Lahore in 1998 and recognized the existence of Pakistan. He realized that the nuclear equation had transformed the region. Dr Manmohan Singh was equally committed to

India. Yet, he tried to explore with President Pervez Musharraf in 2007 how the borders between the two nations could be made irrelevant.

Dr Farooq Abdullah is more Indian than most, yet he has consistently maintained that the geographical de facto between the two countries must be turned into the de jure. That is the only solution.

Whipping Up Jingoism

Prime Minister Modi either does not want to see the reality or all this chest-thumping is for mere domestic consumption. He wants to use the Pakistan card to both raise chauvinistic fervour and polarize people on religious grounds by insinuating and yet not saying that Muslims, whether on this side or that, are unreliable.

It is high time he and his government realized that they are dealing with a bunch of extremely malevolent characters across the border, who may want to test him on his rhetoric through their proxies and non-state actors again and yet again, for they have detected not a chink but a hole in the armour.

In the meanwhile, what happens to the relationship between the two countries. The best-case scenario is no war but no peace. This is the price India continues to unfortunately pay for living in a bad neighbourhood. Can this change? Can a punitive cost be imposed on Pakistan for exporting terror? The answer is yes, but for that you require the calibrated use of a range of diplomatic and deniable options. Breast-beating xenophobia is no fix.

The Quint
18 August 2016

CAN INDIA, PAKISTAN STUMBLE INTO A WAR?

Samay ke bandhano se, paristhitiyon ki aavashyakta se, yudh bhi anivarya ho jata hai (Compulsions of time and the requirements of a situation can render war unavoidable) – thus spoke Narendra Damodardas Modi at a Dussehra event in Lucknow on Tuesday. What are these circumstances and compulsions? Is it only terror or is it something very deeply intrinsic and internally dysfunctional? Consider the following data points that profile a very gloomy spectre.

In 2015, India added the fewest organized-sector jobs in large corporations and manufacturing facilities in seven years across eight core industry sectors. The ratio of jobs in the unorganized sector without monthly payments or social security benefits is set to rise to 93 per cent in 2017. Rural wages are at a decadal low as agriculture, that accounts for 47 per cent of jobs, contracted 0.2 per cent in 2014–15, and grew by 1 per cent in 2015–16. Around 60 per cent of people with jobs don't find employment for the entire year, indicating widespread underemployment and temporary jobs. The formation of companies has slowed to the 2009 levels, and the existing firms are growing at 2 per cent, the lowest in five years. With large corporations and public-sector banks financially stressed, the average size of companies in India is reducing, at a time when well-organized large companies are central to creating jobs.

Without a fundamental transformation in the economy, a basic reset of economic priorities, these jobs will not materialize. The traditional way countries have developed, through low-end manufacturing such as garment exports, and then migrating to higher-end work such as automobiles and electronics, is now passé. Another equally big reason is the lack of trained manpower. This may astonish the urban Indian elite, who can get jobs relatively easily due to their access to reasonably good education. But the vast majority of Indians don't have access to this resource and, therefore, aren't equipped to work in a modern economy. The no-brainer solution, therefore, is to equip millions of people with basic blue-collar skills. Even here, despite the Skill India programme, results will take time as the quality of primary instruction in India is very poor. A period of mass unemployment and social unrest is looming over the immediate horizon unless there is an internal and external shift that at the moment is conspicuous by its absence.

If the World Bank is to be believed, automation threatens 69 per cent of jobs in India and 77 per cent in China, and a whopping 85 per cent in Ethiopia. A recent Bank report underscores that technology could fundamentally disrupt the pattern of the traditional economic path in developing countries. 'As we continue to encourage more investment in infrastructure to promote growth, we also have to think about the kinds of infrastructure that countries will need in the economy of the future. We all know technology has and will continue to fundamentally reshape the world,' says World Bank president Jim Yong Kim. 'But the traditional economic path from increasing productivity of agriculture to light manufacturing and then to full-scale industrialisation may not be possible for all developing countries,' Mr Kim adds.

If this is accurate, and if India is going to lose so many jobs, we have to understand what paths to economic growth are available, and then adapt our approach to asset creation accordingly. Mechanization and technology have disrupted conventional industrial production, upended manual jobs and call time on work that has been done by generations. According to the labour ministry's 27th Quarterly Employment Survey of eight job-intensive industries - textiles, leather, metals, automobiles, gems and jewellery, transport, IT/BPO, and handloom/powerloom - there were 43,000 job losses in the first quarter of 2015-16. There have been no signs of recovery in 2016; in fact, there is a decline.

The monthly economic report for August 2016 by the department of economic affairs underlines these ominous trends. It states overall growth in the index of industrial production (IIP) was - 2.4 per cent in July 2016, in contrast to 4.3 per cent in July 2015. IIP growth during April-July 2016-17 was - 0.2 per cent, compared to 3.5 per cent in the corresponding period last year. It says that merchandise exports and imports declined by 0.3 per cent and 14.1 per cent (in dollar terms) respectively in August 2016 over August 2015. In August 2016, oil imports and non-oil imports declined by 8.5 per cent and 15.6 per cent respectively over August 2015. In April-August 2016, merchandise exports fell 3.0 per cent while merchandise imports fell 15.9 per cent. The rupee appreciated against the US dollar and pound sterling by 0.4 per cent and 0.8 per cent respectively in August 2016 over July 2016. The wholesale price index (WPI) headline inflation increased to 3.7 per cent in August 2016, from 3.5 per cent in July. If you go out into the market, business sentiment is at a nadir, with realty-sector promoters even willing to go to jail rather than honour their obligations. There is blood on the streets; the outlook gloomy, and people are in a real strop.

The run-up to the 2019 general election is going to be worse, with crude prices starting to harden. Oil stood at $51.35 on 10 October 2016. Some analysts claim that oil will hit $120 a barrel by early 2018. If that happens, the Indian economy would be up a creek without a paddle. It doesn't even have the intellectual bandwidth to handle such a volatile economy. The exit of Raghuram Rajan shows how uncomfortable this government is with independent intellect and autonomous action.

Under these circumstances, what would Prime Minister Narendra Modi need to hang onto the coattails of office? He is driven by only one impulse: the insatiable hunger for power. A diversion and a very strong one indeed. There is nothing like a good old war hysteria or even a war to get the passion of raw jingoism gripping the nation. The nuclear overhang be damned.

The Pakistani deep state continues to provide the necessary ingredients for this diversion by its persistent use of semi-state actors against India. It suits Nawaz Sharif to attach himself to the army-ISI-terrorist nexus, given his standing is at an all-time low after the Panama Papers and other exposes. A distinguished analyst with a global think tank who was in Pakistan recently has said Pakistan almost seems like a country coming apart at the seams, making its last stand. Between 2011 and 2015, the Pakistani economy grew by a mere 3.84 per cent on an average. In 2016, it clocked a mere 4.7 per cent and in 2017, it is expected to grow by 5.2 per cent, stagnating at the Lashkar rate of growth. With a public debt of $50 billion, of which around $30 billion was due for repayment in July-September this year, the fact that the Pakistani economy is floundering is a gross understatement.

There is thus a strong incentive on both sides of Wagah to keep the pot boiling, just as Atal Behari Vajpayee did between December 2001 and May 2004. However, he knew the red lines, and that is why he didn't allow the Indian armed forces to cross the Line of Control. With many in the current establishment cocking a snook at the LoC and hysterical right-wingers and certain dubious Pakistanis egging them on, there is a real chance that we may just stumble into a war. If the missiles really flew, there would be little left of the subcontinent. We would have effectively bombed ourselves back into the Stone Age.

The Asian Age
13 October 2016

TALK TO PAK, IT'S NOT A SIGN OF WEAKNESS

At a recent conference on regional security in South Asia, a Pakistani official made a rather startling remark: 'Even if you resolve Kashmir, it does not mean terrorism would stop.' The comment - if it reflects more than an individual opinion - is pregnant with meaning for its sheer portentousness. Does it suggest a shift in the Pakistani deep state's basic philosophy of how it would now use the network of its semi-state actors?

There are two fundamental impulses that drive the Pakistani strategy of bleeding India with a thousand cuts. The first is revenge for the humiliation of Bangladesh and the second is Kashmir.

From 1990 onwards, Pakistan has perpetuated this myth that oppression in Kashmir was motivating young men to wage a proxy war in India. There was a whole host of unemployed fighters from the days of the Afghan jihad against the erstwhile Soviet Union who needed to be redeployed, for their presence in Pakistan was creating problems for social stability within that country and thus Kashmir became the cause of choice.

While Gen. Zia-ul-Haq was credited with evolving the 'bleed India with a thousand cuts' policy and operationalizing it with Punjab as the target in the late 1970s and early 1980s, it was taken to the next level by the powerful director-general of the ISI, the late Hamid Gul.

Gul led the Inter-Services Intelligence (ISI) in 1987-89 and laid the foundations of the violence that hit the Kashmir Valley in the 1990s. Subsequently, Pakistan stepped up the scale of its operations and brought the proxy war to the Indian mainland by the turn of the millennium. However, Kashmir continued to remain the permanent excuse.

What has then changed? Is it that the publicly-acknowledged operations along the LoC on 29 September is making the Pakistanis drop the pretence of Kashmir being the alibi for their depredations? How should India respond to such a situation? There is no difficulty with a tit-for-tat, however intrinsic the risk of uncalibrated escalation might be. Dangers may come due to situations that may have nothing to do with India but can become a trigger.

For instance, the attack on the police academy outside Quetta on 25 October in the restive province of Balochistan. Quetta is also where the Taliban Shura is based. India or its instrumentalities would have had nothing to do with the attack. Despite the high-decibel rhetoric emanating out of India about the situation in Balochistan, India does not believe in fomenting terror; it is not a part of the intrinsic DNA of the Indian state.

However, the statements that have emanated out of responsible establishment figures and the almost hysterical and jingoistic discourse in our media make India a convenient whipping boy. Inspector General of Frontier Corps Maj. Gen. Sher Afghan informed the press that the attackers acted on directions from Afghanistan and the initial investigation suggests the terrorists were affiliated to Lashkar-e-Jhangvi al-Alami, a terror group known to be supported by the Research and Analysis Wing, India's external intelligence agency.

Earlier too on 8 August, the chief minister of the provincial government of Balochistan, Sanaullah Khan Zehri, was quick to blame India for a bomb blast in a Quetta hospital that killed 93 people even before the police could say who was responsible for that horrific attack.

Therefore, even a non-existent tit-for-tat syndrome could

cause an intensification that could quickly spin out of control. Contrary to what some strategic thinkers may believe, there is no space for a limited war between the two countries under a nuclear overhang.

Under such circumstances, talking to each other rather than talking at each other is a sensible strategy. History is replete with examples of nations at war continuing to talk to each other concurrently. It is not a sign of weakness; it is, in fact, a sign of strength.

The most classical example of this perhaps is the talks between the United States and North Vietnam. The war began in 1954. The first major peace proposal from North Vietnamese Premier Pham Van Dong came only 11 years later in April 1965. Even then, there wasn't any significant progress in the negotiations until an informal meeting between Averell Harriman and XuanThuy - the US and North Vietnamese emissaries respectively - took place on 10 May 1968 in Paris.

Even then, peace talks remained frozen for the next four years. South Vietnam at first refused to recognize the sovereignty of the National Liberation Front (NLF) and North Vietnam and vice versa. Once the talks began, each party stated their positions over and over again. The North Vietnamese demanded the US withdraw its troops, dissolve the Saigon government and return to the principles of the Geneva Accords. On the other side, the US insisted on Hanoi recognizing the legitimacy of South Vietnam. Every round of negotiations ended in a stalemate almost as soon as they started.

To deal with this seemingly impossible situation in Paris in August 1969, Nixon directed Henry Kissinger, his national security adviser, to start secret one-on-one meetings with Le Duc Tho, a member of the North Vietnamese politburo. Three years passed by with little progress from both sides. A major breakthrough came on 8 October 1972, when Le Duc Tho and

Henry Kissinger reached an agreement to end the conflict. In late October 1972, Kissinger unveiled a draft of the treaty. Finally, on 27 January 1973, the Paris Peace accord was signed by the US, South and North Vietnam and the NLF.

A full-scale war raging concurrent with the negotiations killed millions of people and saw the extensive use of napalm bombs and other deadly chemical weapons. Ultimately, the war ended, Vietnam was unified in 1976 and barely 27 years later, it rolled out the red carpet for President Bill Clinton in 2000.

If history is any guide, then the various European powers and Great Britain should never be at peace with each other given that they had spent centuries going for each other's throats. Most generals would tell you very few conflicts end in victories on the battlefield and most end up on the negotiating table in armistices. It is, therefore, a wrong notion we have in India that talking to Pakistan is a sign of weakness.

The Asian Age
29 October 2016

WHY JADHAV NEEDS TO BE BROUGHT BACK

As the nation celebrated the 40th anniversary of the Liberation of Bangladesh, I raised the issue of 54 missing Indian prisoners of war (PoWs) in the Lok Sabha on 29 December 2011. They have been in illegal Pakistani captivity since the 1971 war and have never been returned to India. This is despite India returning 91,000 PoWs.

Responding to that special mention, the then External Affairs Minister SM Krishna in a letter acknowledged that there are believed to be 74 missing soldiers, including 54 PoWs, since 1971 languishing in Pakistani jails. However, Pakistan does not acknowledge the presence of any Indian PoWs in its custody.

He further added that the Government of India has repeatedly taken up the issue of missing Indian defence personnel, including PoWs, believed to be in Pakistan, with the Pakistan government through diplomatic channels and during high-level contacts.

During the visit of the then external affairs minister to Pakistan in January 2007, the Pakistani government was persuaded to receive a delegation or relatives of the missing defence personnel to permit them to visit prisons in Pakistan where they are believed to be incarcerated. A delegation of relatives visited 10 jails in Pakistan from 1-14 June 2007, but could not confirm the physical presence of the Indian PoWs.

However, five years later in 2012, a peculiar thing happened. A sepoy of the Punjab Regiment, Jaspal Singh, believed to be dead in the 1971 war, turned up alive in an Omani prison.

He reached out to one Sukhdev Singh, a Punjabi carpenter,

who had gone to Oman on a work visa in 2010. After his return from Oman in July 2012, Sukhdev, a resident of Dugri village in Rupnagar, informed the locals and officials that he was contacted by sepoy Jaspal Singh when he had gone to install kitchen equipment in the prison at Masirah Island.

According to Sukhdev, when he was working in the kitchen, one Punjabi inmate discreetly approached him and gave him details of his village, Pamour, in Fatehgarh Sahib district and said that he was sepoy Jaspal Singh of Punjab Regiment and that he was captured by the Pakistan Army at Hussainiwala near the Ferozepur border along with four more soldiers on 4 December 1971, after which they were all detained in a Pakistani prison for six years before being transferred to the Masirah Island prison in Oman.

Strangely, last month, in March 2017, the Indian embassy in Oman, in reply to an RTI query, disavowed that any Indian national was detained on Masirah Island. Why on earth would Sukhdev spin a yarn like this? Why did we not follow up on Jaspal? If the person Sukhdev met in that island prison was not Jaspal, then who he was. Is he still there or has he disappeared? Why is the silence of the government deafening?

Then there is the case of Sarabjit Singh, who was murdered by the Pakistanis in Kot Lakhpat jail in Lahore on 2 May 2013, despite a very high-decibel and passionate campaign by his sister Dalbir Kaur for his release that had massive support among the liberals even in Pakistan.

Now turning to Kulbhushan Jadhav, the news about his death sentence came as a bolt from the blue. Ostensibly, a Pakistani military court in some sham legal proceedings tried him and handed down the death penalty. Pakistani Army Chief Qamar Javed Bajwa, in some rather abnormal hurry, has confirmed the same. This is notwithstanding the fact that Sartaj Aziz, the foreign affairs adviser to the Pakistani prime minister, told members of the Pakistani Senate on 8 December 2016: 'What the dossier contained on Indian spy KulbhushanYadav were mere statements. It did not have any conclusive evidence.'

What has changed between then and now, given the fact that Mr Aziz does not have a reputation of either shooting from the mouth or the hip? Does this kneejerk confirmation by the Pakistan Army Chief have something to do with the alleged disappearance of retired Lt Col Mohammad Habib Zahir of the Pakistan Army in Nepal a few days ago as is being widely speculated on the social and mainstream media?

The other thing that seems to be fairly evident is that Jadhav was not arrested from Mashkel, Balochistan as was claimed by Pakistan. A theory that has been going around for a while is that Jadhav's abduction is somehow linked to the action taken by the Indian Coast Guard against a Pakistani boat on the night of 31 December 2014. While reports in the Indian media suggested that this was another attempt by Pakistan to orchestrate a 26/11 kind of operation, which could be true, what is also speculated is that the boat belonged to a notorious Pakistani smuggler who, in retaliation for the gutting of his boat by the Indian Coast Guard, kidnapped Jadhav and handed him over to the ISI for monetary or other considerations.

While all this would remain in the realm of conjecture, what is uncontroverted is that Jadhav is a retired Indian naval officer who unfortunately is in a very life-threatening situation, and it is our responsibility as a nation to do everything to bring him home safe and sound.

What are the legal options available to him? Frankly, none. Theoretically, he can appeal to the Military Appellate Tribunal and then even to the Pakistan Supreme Court followed by a clemency petition to the President of Pakistan. However, in such matters, even the court and the President would just end up toeing the line of the establishment. Insofar as the Military

Appellate Tribunal is concerned, the less said the better.

Only two things will work: one 'maybe' and the other 'perhaps'. The 'maybe' option is that India mounts a shrill high-decibel international campaign to secure his release. This would entail the involvement of inter-governmental organizations such as the International Committee of the Red Cross, United Nations Human Rights Council, other UN instrumentalities and even organizations like Amnesty International that this government does not really fancy. However, given the manner in which the Pakistanis have played even the Americans over Osama bin Laden and still continue to have a fairly decent relationship with them, it is doubtful whether they will care more than a fig about the international community.

The 'perhaps' option is for Prime Minister NarendraModi to pick up the phone and speak to Nawaz Sharif directly and tell him in no uncertain terms that such kangaroo court verdicts are simply unacceptable. The Indian high commission in Pakistan should also concurrently reach out to moderate sections of society, lawyers, and other human rights activists, to start a campaign within that country for his release.

India should make Jadhav a test case of its resolve to get our fellow citizen back home. Let him not end up like the 54 PoWs, alive but forgotten, or like Sarabjit Singh, brutally murdered. Let no partisan politics divide us.

The Asian Age
15 April 2017

MEDIA INITIATIVES CAN BETTER INDIA-PAK TIES

On Monday, 24 July, at 3 pm Eastern Standard Time (12.30 am IST) Senator Mushahid Hussain, the former information minister of Pakistan, and I will sit down for a public conversation at the Atlantic Council in Washington D.C. The objective is to examine the role played by media narratives in the relationship between India and Pakistan.

At a point in time when relations between the two nations have touched a nadir, cross-border shelling and raids are more the norm than the exception, dominant national narratives in both India and Pakistan only fuel further tensions with media platforms – print, broadcasting and social media – amplifying the stereotyping and underscoring the otherness of the other. The idea is to explore the possibility of a way forward in the relationship given all the known knowns.

Can our syncretic though strained cultural intertwining be reimagined and reinvigorated, for conflict should not be the new normal. Does the media have a role – other than that of a spoiler – to play in this paradigm?

Before addressing this question, let me briefly outline the structure of media in both countries. In India, the total number of registered publications, as on 31 March 2016, for which the Registrar of Newspapers for India (RNI) figures are available was 1,10,851. The number of newspapers was 16,136 and periodicals 94,715. The combined circulation of all print publications during the year 2015-16 was 61,02,38,581. The breakdown of circulation numbers was as follows: Hindi publications – 31,44,55,106; English publications – 6,54,13,443 and Urdu publications 5,17,75,006.

The total number of private television channels as on 31 May 2017, was 882. Out of these 391 are news channels and 491 are general entertainment channels. And 183 million homes have access to cable and satellite television. The total number of private FM radio stations are 243 and there are 200 operational community radio stations. The number of Internet users has touched 465 million as of June 2017. In addition to that public broadcaster Prasar Bharati runs an elaborate radio and television network.

In Pakistan also the media landscape is equally rich and diverse. 140 million people have direct or communal access to television with approximately 15 million cable TV connections being shared by 105 million viewers. There are 105 private satellite television channels that have been licenced by the Pakistan Electronic Media Regulatory Authority (PEMRA). In addition to this, state broadcaster Pakistan TV runs its own terrestrial network. There are 269 medium wave, short wave and FM radio stations with a listenership of 190 million people; of these 96 are private FM radio stations. There are 3,080 print publications in Pakistan, including 457 registered newspapers and 2,623 periodicals. Out of the 457, 195 are Urdu newspapers, 161 Sindhi, 98 English and three are in Gujarati. Pakistan has 34 million Internet users out of which 3.1 million have broadband Internet connectivity as of July 2016. The numbers must have gone up in the past year.

It is therefore quite evident that with such widespread proliferation of private media there is scope to write a new script for the India-Pakistan relationship. Then where is the problem? The media and public opinion have a had an intricate correlation – a typical chicken and egg situtation.

States routinely use the media to propagate a certain narrative, fly trial balloons prior to formulating a policy and even rally public opinion to provide the rationale for a particular policy decision. The flip side of this manipulation is that states themselves become hostages to the perceptions they create through the media when they want to shift gears of policymaking. This is a truism insofar as India and Pakistan are concerned given that the anti-India sentiment in Pakistan and anti-Pakistan mawkishness across the border are seen as both patriotic and nationalistic in both countries.

Then there has been a fertile field of trauma, conflict, bitterness and odium dating back to 1947, that has only got exacerbated as passed-on memories from generation to generation have amplified the villainous and rapacious credentials of the other without ever emphasising the commonalities and shared heritage. To that has been added the antagonism of the past 70 years.

One good effort was made under the aegis of the Aman ki Asha programme. It was conceived and implemented jointly by two media houses, one from India and the other from Pakistan. Launched on 1 January 2010, it endeavoured to facilitate normalisation of relations through a three-pronged strategy, first being the resolution of disputes through dialogue and discussion. They would bring members of governments, hawks, international think tanks and civil society on their print and electronic media platforms to discuss complex issues that continue to bedevil the two countries and propose solutions. Second, to bring leaders of industry together and propose resumption of trade and investment, given that mutual economic benefit could be the strongest binding force of good bilateral relations. Third, to encourage greater people-to-people contacts through increased cultural exchanges.

Over a period of three years, between 2010 and 2013, Aman ki Asha caught the fancy of people in both countries. It was applauded by the international community and was affirmed as the 'most likely to thrive' initiative for peace between nuclear-armed India and Pakistan.

However, Aman ki Asha faced opposition from the usual bunch of hyper-nationalists on both sides. The maximum damage was inflicted by a television channel of the same media group that was a partner in the endeavour. While they did Aman ki Asha in the morning their own TV channel made 'Aman ki Ashes' out of it in the evening during 2010-2014.

In Pakistan initially, the deep state supported Aman ki Asha, even facilitated visas for the Indians who came to participate in events sponsored by the peace initiative. However, by 2013, Aman ki Asha was labelled as anti-Pakistan.

A large part of this campaign of innuendo against Aman ki Asha had everything to do with the fact that it was seen as an initiative of two large media houses to the exclusion of others. The other media houses worked overtime to undermine and discredit it, specially in Pakistan. Corporate rivalry trumped a noble initiative to try and build a new narrative between the two countries.

Given the vibrant nature of private media in both countries, a pan-media platform involving as many media players as possible must be created again to resuscitate the initiative albeit on a larger scale. This exertion must go on irrespective of the state of relations at any particular point in time.

In the short and medium term, this effort must focus on the co-production of content. Such collaborative programmes should deal with non-contentious issues – cultural, social, environmental and even economic – that have a bearing on both countries, along with entertainment shows. A viable starting point for the broadcast of such content would be through digital platforms and gradually such shows can be aired simultaneously in both countries on established television channels via satellite links, with identifiable, well-known anchors and guests from both countries.

In the long run, the free and uninterrupted circulation of Indian and Pakistani newspapers, books and other published material across the respective borders and the possibility of directly downlinking Indian and Pakistani news and entertainment channels on either side as well as investments in each other's media industry will help people realise that those on the other side of the border are just like them, have similar hopes, dreams and aspirations. If this movement generates sufficient momentum it would compel even the 'deep state' mandarins to change their spots. For nothing can stop history on the march.

South Asia is home to two billion people. It is the most unconnected region in the world with the worst human development indices. The problem is the India-Pakistan paradigm. We owe it to posterity to surmount our issues and build a better tomorrow for the generations that will come after us.

The Asian Age
22 July 2017

Chinese Chequers

OBOR IS THE GRANDEST FAILURE OF INDIAN FOREIGN POLICY

As the Narendra Modi government completes three years of its tryst with electoral destiny on May 16, it could not have wished for a more portentous international conference in the faraway yet nearby Beijing.

The One Belt One Road conference convened by the People's Republic of China over the weekend to unveil and showcase the most ambitious connectivity project of modern times represents the grandest failure of Indian foreign policy and its quarantine into splendid isolation. However, first a word about the project.

Chinese president Xi Jinping, in 2013, unveiled a novel economic structure that would connect China's Silk Road Mercantile Belt project in Central Asia with its Maritime Silk Road, through linked bodies of water from the South China Sea to the Indian Ocean. In principle, these trade stratagems centre on increasing China's connection with countries along the ancient Silk Road in Eurasia, while creating a new Silk Road across Asia to South Asia and Africa.

One part of the project is focused on the creation of road connections between China and Eurasia, involving infrastructure projects such as highways and rail links. The other part of the project concerns maritime routes that will connect China with South East Asia, South Asia and ports up and down the east coast of Africa.

The measure of this concept, if it ever reaches fruition, is both the project's greatest hawking point and conceivable trial. The trade links once established will cover 65 per cent of the world's population, one-third of global GDP and a quarter of all goods and services in the international economy.

Such a focus on goods and services will upturn how conventional products, such as energy, are traded. Observers draw parallels with the Marshall Plan that reinvented Europe after the Second World War. With enormous sums of money, ranging from $800 billion to $1 trillion to be invested over the next five years, there is a lot of cash to spread around, even in China's extended neighbourhood.

In comparison, the investment into the Pakistani component of this initiative, the Chinese Pakistan Economic Corridor (CPEC), anywhere between $46-62 billion, is a mere pittance.

The summit in Beijing over the weekend was attended by 29 heads of state and government which included Pakistani Prime Minister Nawaz Sharif, Sri Lankan Prime Minister Ranil Wickremesinghe, delegations from all other South Asian countries barring Bhutan, as well as leaders and officials from the big players on the global stage – Russia, US, Japan, UK, Germany and France.

That is where India's lack of nimbleness became counterproductive. While our objection to the CPEC is extremely valid – that it passes through territory acceded to India by the erstwhile Maharaja of Jammu and Kashmir, Hari Singh, on 26 October 1947 and whatever is in the possession of Pakistan is illegally Occuoied – the moot point remains that we were not able to carry any of the big powers, including the US, and especially our neighbours along on the vital question of Westphalian sovereignty.

By boycotting the summit rather than showing up and

making our voice heard loud and clear in the comity of nations, India has in fact sent out a message that it will make proforma noise on this issue but actually acquiesce to the fait accompli.

What this lack of dexterity does is allow the Chinese embrace of Pakistan to get even tighter. A front-page exclusive in Pakistan's *Dawn* newspaper for the first time revealed to Pakistanis themselves the extent of Chinese colonisation this project would entail. But given the desperate, if not perilous, situation that Pakistan finds itself in, it would be surprising if there is any substantive protest by any section of the population.

A strategic relationship transformed into an economic vested interest means that India cannot bank upon Chinese neutrality in case of a possible conflict with Pakistan - which India may blunder into as the BJP-led government works overtime to use the Kashmir flashpoint to drive home the otherness of the citizens to the rest of India.

A two-front situation may become an unfortunate imperative that India may just have to deal with, given the fact that China is revising its position on accepted principles with regard to the territorial dispute with India, in the protracted but ongoing Special Representative process.

With Gwadar Port becoming operational, China would be able to surmount its Malacca Dilemma by transporting its energy and mineral resources directly to Kashgar as they exit the Straits of Hormuz — thereby circumventing the Malacca chokepoint.

The fact remains that India would have to deal with Pakistani and Chinese navies jointly patrolling the Arabian Sea off India's western seaboard and directly threatening India's energy and resource supply lines. The story does not end there. With Hambantota also being developed as a Chinese-resourced port in Sri Lanka, the Gwadar-Hambantota axis may end up emerging as an access denial area in India's home waters.

Then there is the eastern headache, which is the growing Chinese proximity to Nepal and Bangladesh, as well as the deep economic linkages with Myanmar. While Sheikh Hasina's government is very friendly towards India, that may not be the permanent state of play. There is a perception in the Bangladesh polity, especially the principal opposition Bangladesh Nationalist Party (BNP), that India has put all its eggs in one basket.

Given the strained relations with Nepal since the economic blockade of 2015, Kathmandu's propensity to explore other options especially energises the torturous land route with China.

While all this infrastructure development has been in the works for a while, where the Modi government has tripped badly is in its inability to tread the fine balance between the big powers. Though its perceived cosiness towards the US has not borne any tangible fruit in the past three years, what it has achieved is drive both Russia and China into a state of ambivalence and antagonism, respectively. There is no better evidence of this than the recent Russian-Pakistani defense exercises, a first in 70 years.

It is therefore in India's larger national interest to not allow the China-Pakistan embrace to turn into its greatest strategic nightmare. India must finesse its relationship with China, for there are other implications, namely in Afghanistan.

This is only one of the great blunders over the past three years. The others will follow in the days to come.

The Indian Express
16 May 2017

AS INDIA-CHINA STANDOFF CONTINUES, ABSENCE OF FULL-TIME DEFENCE MINISTER IS GLARING

Chinese president Xi Jinping refused to meet Prime Minister Narendra Modi in a structured bilateral meeting on the margins of the G20 summit in Hamburg over the weekend, though reports suggest that they had a 'pull aside' conversation.

The Chinese had categorically ruled out a 'one-on-one' meeting, citing the standoff in the Doklam area near the Bhutan tri-junction for the past 19 days. (Doka La is the Indian name for the region that Bhutan knows as Doklam while China asserts that it is a part of its Donglang region.) Given the fact that less than 34 months ago, in September 2014, Modi was personally serenading Xi on the banks of the Sabarmati River in Ahmedabad, it calls for a deep dive to discern why the Sino-Indian relationship has reached such a pass. Is the deterioration in the relationship sudden or was it sliding steadily and surreptitiously hidden from the public gaze ?

Here's an incident that is believed to have taken place when Modi visited Xian, Xi's hometown, in May 2015. Apparently, the prime minister raised the matter of the unsettled border issue, expressing concern over the slow pace of the Special Representative process between the two countries. The response from the Chinese side was illuminating. They, evidently, told him that there are three segments of the border - Northern (Chinese Western) where India needs to sort out issues with Pakistan and only then would the Chinese talk about that sector; the Central (Middle), where the border is relatively settled; and the Eastern (Chinese Eastern), which India calls Arunachal Pradesh and the Chinese refer to as South Tibet, where substantive outstanding issues needs to be dealt with. In other words India should relinquish its claim on Arunachal Pradesh.

The reason this piece of minutiae is important is the current point of impasse is almost at the end of the Central (Middle) sector and the beginning of the Eastern sector where, even according to the Chinese, there were no major irritants even 26 months ago. This stretches from Himachal Pradesh to the Eastern end of the state of Sikkim. Even though the current standoff is in Bhutanese territory, the Chinese are not blind to the 'special' relationship between India and Bhutan.

During a 2012 interaction with leaders of political parties from across Asia in Beijing, a Chinese Communist Party apparatchik on the cusp of a major leadership elevation outlined China's three objectives over the next decade: to transform China from a low-income to a middle-income country, to move manufacturing facilities further into the hinterland from the coastal regions and to consolidate individual grassroots democracy across the country. China, he said, needed another three decades of peace to properly fulfill this vision. Moreover, he emphasized, the rise of China in Asia would be peaceful.

Although China's conduct with regard to Japan over the Senkaku Islands in the East China Sea or generally with the other littoral states of the South China Sea has been acerbic and belligerent, there is another dimension to the Chinese behaviour that should not be ignored. To the exclusion of its territorial disputes with India and Bhutan, China has settled all its other land boundary disputes. In contrast, it has resolved none of its maritime border disputes, with the honourable exception of the Gulf of Tonkin dispute with Vietnam, that was partially resolved after protracted negotiations spanning three rounds – in 1974, 1978-1979 and 1992-2000.

China-watchers are bemused and a tad intrigued at the territorial concessions that China has repeatedly given to resolve its myriad conflicts. Of its 23 ongoing territorial disputes from 1949, China proposed generous concessions in as many as 17, often agreeing to receive less than half the land it initially claimed. A classical example is the Sino-Tajik border dispute that was settled by an agreement between the two countries in January 2011. The agreement that resolved a 130-year-old territorial dispute, required Tajikistan to cede around 1,000 square kilometers of land in the Pamir Mountains to China. It mandates that China will receive only 3.5 per cent of the 28,000 sq kms of land it had asked for by declaring it as historical Chinese lands. While, under its boundary settlements with Kazakhstan and Kyrgyzstan, China settled for just 22 and 32 per cent respectively of the land it had disputed, respectively.

This situation then begs the obvious question: Why have the Sino-Indian border talks not made progress? In April 2016, after a meeting of the Special Representatives, the Chinese foreign ministry came out with an interestingly quixotic formulation. The statement put out by the Chinese said, 'Starting from the big picture of long-term development of bilateral relations, both sides will, with the positive attitude of mutual respect and understanding and on the basis of existing results from negotiations, stay on the track of political settlement, stick to peaceful negotiations to resolve the boundary question, meet each other halfway and continue to promote the process of framework negotiation so as to strive for a fair and reasonable solution that both sides accept.' Significantly this offer to meet halfway came one year after the PM's apparent dissatisfaction on the matter in Xian.

Settlement of territorial questions involves land swaps which requires political will. Given the fact that the 1962 wound is regularly dredged out and given an airing which has not allowed this injury to the 'collective Indian psyche' to heal, notwithstanding the 1967 border clashes in Nathu La when the Indian Army gave the Chinese a bloody nose, as well as in Sumdorong Chu in 1986 when the Indians checkmated the Chinese. But we tend to forget all this and are obsessed with a sense of victimhood.

The Chinese have sensed this lack of political will in the current Indian leadership, despite all the grandstanding and bluster, and possibly feel that India being a traditional status quo power would not want to change the de jure for that would involve changing the facts on the ground. That is why they have decided to probe Prime Minister Modi even in an area that has for long been tranquil.

India's refusal to participate in Xi Jinping's OBOR (One Belt One Road) fantasy and the fact that only little Bhutan stood with India on boycotting that conference has underscored New Delhi's isolation to the Chinese even in the neighbourhood while singling out Bhutan for Chinese fire. Coupled with that is the larger Asian canvas. The Asian power dynamic consists of the interplay between the US that considers itself to be an Asian power, Russia, China, Japan and India. It is a dynamic that has to be finessed very subtly. Unfortunately the current government has tripped badly. While it has not got anything substantive out of the US-Japan-India strategic trilateral despite the soon-to-commence Operation Malabar in the Bay of Bengal, featuring three aircraft carriers from all these three countries, it has lost both Russia and China. The Russians, despite their protestations, have supped with the Pakistanis and the dragon is breathing fire on the trijunction of Bhutan, China and India.

India does not have the luxury of being separated by two oceans from China. It also has had a positive relationship with it notwithstanding the boundary question over the past three decades after Prime Minister Rajiv Gandhi's momentous visit to China in 1988.

Prime Minister Modi would be well advised not to let TV anchors and their panelists masquerade as Indian public opinion. The equilibrium in the relationship with China needs to be restored through quiet old-world diplomacy, while continuing to work with the US and Russia to build our military capacity and capabilities that have woefully been neglected by the current government.

Nothing underlines it more than the fact that India does not have a full time Defence Minister. As for the 'political will to settle outstanding territorial issues', the less said the better.

The Indian Express
10 July 2017

DOKLAM: LESSONS FROM 1962

On the 11th of August at 1659 IST that corresponds to 7.29 AM Eastern Standard Time, President Donald Trump tweeted, 'Military Solutions are now fully in place, locked and loaded, should North Korea act unwisely. Hopefully Kim Jong-un will find another path. He followed it up by retweeting the US Pacific Command that said its B-1B Lancer bombers on Guam, that are armed with Nuclear weapons stand ready to fulfill United States Forces Korea's Fight Tonight mission.

The tweet was in response to the North Korean leader Kim Jong-un's rather bellicose rhetoric threatening to launch four intermediate-range ballistic missiles into waters near Guam in the Western Pacific to teach President Trump a lesson, after the president warned of 'fire and fury' against Pyongyang if it persisted in threatening the United States. Guam is unincorporated United States territory situated in Micronesia in the Western Pacific Ocean. General Kim Rak-gyom is the commander of the Strategic Rocket Forces of the North Korean People's Army charged with executing the rather apocalyptic vision that nation has for that part of Asia.

Guess who blinked first in this escalating war of words? Not Trump, not Kim Jong-un but Xi Jingping the Chinese President. In a phone call the very next day to President Trump he counseled patience. Xi reportedly said, 'At present, relevant parties should exercise restraint and avoid words and actions that would escalate tensions on the Korean Peninsula.'

Now contrast this with the Chinese behaviour on Doklam. Ever since the Chinese intruded into Bhutanese territory on the pretext of building a road, and the Indian troops prevented them from doing so, the Chinese have been bellicose, belligerent and downright obtuse in their statements towards India. Perhaps never before have the Chinese used such ugly language in their public interaction with India. The response of the Indian government has been a studied silence. Suddenly all the bluster and arrogance that have been the trademark of this government for the past 38 months seem to have disappeared down the tube.

Sample some of the Chinese statements: 'Such rhetoric is extremely irresponsible. We hope (the) particular person in the Indian Army could learn from historical lessons and stop such clamouring for war.' This was in response to the Chief of the Indian Army saying that India was ready to take on China, Pakistan and the internal security challenges concurrently. Then the Chinese upped the ante further and called the External Affairs Minister of India a liar. An editorial in China's state-controlled *Global Times* said, 'Indian Foreign Minister Sushma Swaraj told her country's parliament on Thursday that 'all countries are in India's support,"' and said India is alert to the need to protect its securi... She was lying to the parliament.' It further said, 'First, India's invasion of Chinese territory is a plain fact... Second, India's military strength is far behind that of China.'

On India's Independence Day, Chinese and Indian forces clashed in Eastern Ladakh north of the Pangong Tso (lake). Both armies pelted stones at each other that left people injured on both sides. Late last month, 10-15 PLA soldiers had 'transgressed' almost one km into a disputed pocket – a mutually agreed 'demilitarized zone' – at Barahoti in the Chamoli district of Uttarakhand twice in quick succession.

Where is this government erring in its engagement with the Chinese? While it is true that the Chinese beat us in 1962, it is equally correct that India gave China a bloody nose in 1967 at

Nathu La. Again in 1986 by executing Operation Falcon, India outsmarted the Chinese by taking up aggressive positions on the Hathung La ridge overlooking Sumdorong Chu along with other key mountain features beyond Twang in Arunachal Pradesh. India also deployed T-72 tanks and infantry combat vehicles in the Demchok area of Ladakh and northern Sikkim forcing the Chinese to back off from the aggressive territorial claims they had started making in the Eastern Sector where China claims the border question is the most convoluted.

Even in 1962 India was let down by its friends, especially the erstwhile Soviet Union that virtually allowed the Chinese to go ahead with the aggression against India in return for verbal solidarity during the Cuban Missile Crisis. Again, in 1966 Prime Minister Lal Bahadur Shastri passed away under rather mysterious circumstances in Tashkent (erstwhile USSR). It was the United States of America that came to India's aid during the most challenging time – the Chinese aggression of 1962. Though the Soviet Union more than made all that up during the 1971 war that led to the creation of Bangladesh. The Soviet Eastern Fleet slipped anchor in Vladivostok as the American Seventh Fleet steamed into the Bay of Bengal.

Writing for the Cold War International History Project Bulletin 251 on the basis of archival material made available after the collapse of the erstwhile Soviet Union, MY Prozumenschikov explains the situation in 1962 leading up to the Sino-Indian conflict: 'The situation changed on October 22, when the speech of US President John F Kennedy effectively put a tough choice before Khrushchev: conflict, with likely use of nuclear weapons, or retreat. The first scenario threatened the whole world with catastrophe; the second was acutely painful for the USSR and its leader. Searching for a way out, Moscow, in the midst of everything, turned its attention to Beijing. The experience of recent years made it possible for Khrushchev to hope that, at this critical moment in the battle with international imperialism, China would at least momentarily "close its eyes" to the discord and steadfastly support any Soviet action. That had occurred (at least on the surface) in 1956 during the crises in Hungary and Poland, and in 1961 during the Berlin crisis. For his part, Khrushchev was ready to compromise with Mao on a whole series of issues, including the Sino-Indian conflict.

On 25 October, with war with the United States potentially imminent, the newspaper *Pravda* published a front-page article, which had been approved by the CC CPSU, essentially rejecting the position that Moscow had maintained during the course of the whole Sino-Indian border conflict. The article called the McMahon line, which New Delhi accepted, *notorious*, the result of British imperialism, and consequently legally invalid. Moreover, having made this assertion on the eve of the execution of Chinese plans to settle the conflict, *Pravda* also accused India of being incited by imperialists and being the main ringleaders of the conflict and charged that the CPI was sliding toward chauvinism to the detriment of proletarian internationalism.

Moscow's unexpected and abrupt reversal – clearly intended as a gesture to shore up the all but moribund Sino-Soviet alliance in the event of war with the West – provoked a sharp reaction, but not exactly the one that the Soviet leadership had expected. From the documents at TSKHSD, it is clear that the article came as a bombshell, especially in India. Nehru declared that he was very pained by the article, which caused significant damage to India's friendship with the USSR.'

It is thus fairly evident that the Chinese had a cast-iron assurance from the Soviets that their backs were covered when they decided to open a front with India in 1962. There would be no activity on the Sino-Soviet border to the detriment of China.

The situation is somewhat similar in 2017. While there is no Soviet Union today and no Cuban Missile Crisis, there are escalating tensions on the Korean Peninsula. While there are reports in the Indian press about an elevated strategic partnership between India and the US with China as the mark. This may be nothing more than hot air. Anyone familiar with Washington D.C. knows how distracted the US administration is. The possibility of a deal where China leans on North Korea (it's the other client state the first being Pakistan) to roll back it's strategic programe in return for the US looking away on the Sino-Indian border is always within the preponderance of probability. Coupled with that are the contacts between influential Chinese oligarchs and Trump's charmed circle.

Unlike India that was born out of a pacifist freedom struggle the current communist state came into existence as a result of a violent civil war that finally culminated in 1949. China only understands raw power. Given the global power dynamics that India has not been able to finesse, if the push comes to a shove India may have to fight alone.

The Asian Age
2 September 2017

TRUTH ABOUT DOKLAM

On 28 August the ministry of external affairs put out a statement: 'In recent weeks, India and China have maintained diplomatic communication in respect of the incident at Doklam. During these communications, we were able to express our views and convey our concerns and interests. On this basis, expeditious disengagement of border personnel at the face-off site at Doklam has been agreed to and is on-going.'

The first part of the statement made it very clear that through diplomatic channels India had conveyed its concerns and worries about the face-off at Doklam between the forces of the two countries. It further stated that on the basis of this diplomatic exchange expeditious disengagement of troops at the border had been agreed to and was underway. What the statement did not mention was whether the withdrawal was mutual or unilateral by India? What it also did not disclose was whether China had given any explicit or even implicit assurances that they would not construct a road in Doklam – the trigger for the original flashpoint on 18 June.

Now let us turn to what China had to say on the issue.

Responding to a question on the same day as the Indian statement, the spokesperson of China's foreign ministry said, 'We have learned that on the afternoon of 28 August, the Indian border troops and equipment that illegally crossed the Sikkim sector of the China-India border have all been withdrawn to the Indian side, marking an end to the trespassing incident.

'Do you have more information?' The questioner asked.

'On 18 June, the Indian border troops illegally crossed the well-delimited China-India border in the Sikkim sector into

China's Dong Lang area. China has lodged representations with the Indian side many times through diplomatic channels, made the facts and truth of this situation known to the international community, clarified China's solemn position and explicit demands, and urged India to immediately pull back its border troops to the Indian side. In the meantime, the Chinese military has taken effective counter-measures to ensure the territorial sovereignty and legitimate rights and interests of the state. At about 2.30 pm of 28 August, the Indian side withdrew all its border personnel and equipment that were illegally on the Chinese territory to the Indian side. The Chinese personnel onsite have verified this situation. China will continue fulfilling its sovereign rights to safeguard territorial sovereignty in compliance with the stipulations of the border-related historical treaty.'

Another question put to the spokesperson was: 'The Indian government's announcement (talks about) a "mutual disengagement" of the troops between the two countries. You haven't mentioned the pullback of the Chinese troops. You mentioned only the pullback of the Indian troops. How do you explain?'

The spokesperson replied saying, 'The Chinese side has made it clear that the Indian border personnel and equipment that trespassed into China's territory have all been withdrawn to the Indian side of the border. The Chinese border troops continue with their patrols and stationing in the Dong Lang area. China will continue with its exercise of sovereign rights to protect territorial sovereignty in accordance with the stipulations of the border-related historical treaty.'

In response to a further probe the spokesperson reiterated, 'I want to stress that the Indian side withdrew all its border personnel and equipment that were illegally on the Chinese territory to the Indian side. The Chinese personnel onsite have verified this situation. The Chinese border troops continue with their patrols and stationing in the Dong Lang area. China will continue fulfilling its sovereign rights to safeguard territorial sovereignty in compliance with the stipulations of the border-related historical treaty. In the meantime, in light of the changing landscape on the ground, China will make necessary adjustments and deployment as it sees fit.'

The very next day, the Chinese spokesperson again responded to a journalistic query about whether China has stopped building roads in the Dong Lang area. He said that China has said clearly that China has long been carrying out infrastructure building, including roads, in the Dong Lang area to meet the needs of guarding the border and to improve the living and working conditions of the troops stationed there and people living there. 'Taking into account various factors such as weather, we will make proper building plans in the light of the actual situation,' he added.

The Chinese account of the situation has not yet been controverted by any of the Indian officials. What has emerged is that China disavowed that the disengagement was mutual. The Chinese spokesperson's remarks also mention that their border troops continue with their patrols and stationing in the Donglang area. Note the word stationing. In layman's terms it means staying put. The remarks are also ambiguous, to put it rather mildly, about the Chinese road-building plans in the Doklam area. It may just be appropriate to point out that what China calls Dong Lang, Bhutan refers to as Doklam and we as Doka La. A Sino-Indian confrontation is not in the interest of either country and certainly not in the interest of the larger Indo-Pacific region. It may have been wise to ignore the high decibel rhetoric emanating from the Chinese side over the past two months or so.

Clearly, the sudden spurt in Chinese activity in the Doklam

region was connected to the boycott of the One Belt One Road (OBOR) conference by India. Bhutan was the only country out of the region that stood by India and did not attend the high-profile meet.

However, off the record, government sources have told the media that the reason India has chosen to ignore the latest assertions by the Chinese foreign office is to give them a 'face-saver'. Is this a face-saver or an abject surrender?

If indeed we were prepared to swallow our pride, get egg on our face, allow China to grandstand on the global stage and see off the Prime Minister on his way to Xiamen in China for the BRICS summit, then doubts would arise. If China was wrong and we were right, why are we walking the extra nine yards to let China off the hook? That too at a time when it was in China's interest to lower tensions in Doklam as they were facing an almost two-front situation with the Korean peninsula threatening to flare up?

Will China interpret India's magnanimity as a gesture of good faith or a sign of weakness? Will they conclude that the bombastic rhetoric of muscular nationalism spouted over the past three years was the handiwork of people who turned out to have feet of clay when push came to shove? The jury is out on that.

Deccan Chronicle
2 September 2017

The World in a Flux

THE POST-9/11 CHAOS

Libyan leader Muammar Gaddafi was toppled on 23 August 2011, after the National Transitional Council took control of Bab al-Azizia. He was lynched to death on 20 October 2011, in Sirte, his hometown, as his rivals took control of the city.

Yemen's President Ali Abdullah Saleh signed the Gulf Cooperation Council (GCC) power transfer deal in which a presidential election was held, leading to his successor Abd al-Rab Mansur al-Hadi formally replacing him as President on 27 February 2012, in exchange for immunity from prosecution.

However, has anything really changed in the intervening years? Has the world become a safer place after the post-9/11 domino chain of events? The answer is 'no'. In fact, it's now a much more dangerous place with ISIS and other non-state actors gaining clout. By the middle of 2015, Europe was besieged. Millions were on the march. They were fleeing to its shores, escaping the depravity of civil wars in Afghanistan, Iraq, Syria, southeast Turkey, Yemen, Libya, Somalia, Sudan and northeast Nigeria.

Syria and Libya have almost ceased to exist as nation states that cartography comprehends them to be. Half of the 23 million Syrians have become homeless and are seeking refuge. ISIS has rendered another three million Iraqi refugees. Another 1.5 million have been displaced in South Sudan. The multitudes still continue to cross the sea separating West Asia and Africa from Europe in leaky little boats, risking their lives, for their choice is between the devil back home and the deep blue sea they must navigate to reach safety.

America's endeavour to reorder the geography of West Asia, frozen by the Sykes-Picot agreement after the dismemberment of the Ottoman Empire, has failed. It has unleashed such tectonic forces of ethnicity, discontent and hate-fuelled narratives of historic injustices that the entire region from the Hindukush to the Bosphorus Strait and beyond into Arab North Africa is roiling in turmoil.

The fact that the US invasion of Iraq was planned long before 9/11 is now no secret and is extensively documented. The Project for the New American Century - a think tank that included key members of the subsequent Bush administration - had written a letter to President Bill Clinton as early as 26 January 1998, urging regime change in Iraq. Though Mr Obama came to office trying to make a distinction between the bad war (Iraq) and the good war (Afghanistan), he wasn't averse to holding off action against ISIS long enough to build pressure for the ouster of Iraqi PM Nouri Kamal al-Maliki.

What is also missed in the bewildering array of intrigues that runs concurrent to violence are the larger implications of Russia's intervention in Syria. Perhaps, after the disastrous Soviet occupation of Afghanistan, this is the first time Russia has ventured beyond its near abroad. With Istanbul now cosying up to Moscow, the dynamics are fast changing for Turkey, despite it being the eastern anchor of the NATO alliance. It was never included in the European Union as it was a secular Muslim state moving towards Islamism, which made the EU's core quite uneasy.

While Europe has been able to reconcile the wars between the Christian states from Westphalia till the Second World War, they found it subliminally harder to surmount the clash of cultures and civilizations as underscored by the siege of the imperial city of Vienna, seat of the Hapsburg dynasty, by the Ottoman Turks in 1683 and their earlier depredations in Europe.

Among all these strands of history enmeshed in modern hugger-mugger, India would do well to wait and watch rather than walk headlong into paradigms like the US-Afghanistan-India trilateral and the other foundational agreements this government is rushing into. All these agreements were on the backburner for good reasons.

With an election in the US less than two months away, the former First Lady-turned-Senator from New York-turned Secretary of State and now Democratic candidate may want to reassess the corrosive US legacy in the region over the past decade and a half to reset priorities. If it is Donald Trump in the White House, a large part of the world may want to kiss their posterior goodbye...

The Asian Age

17 September 2016

WORLD NEEDS A SHIFT TO A FAIRER DEAL FOR THE 99 PER CENT

Far from the cacophony of television-generated hysteria around Assembly election results in India, a bunch of global thought leaders gathered in Berlin to craft a grand strategy to overcome the new authoritarian right-wing populism that has been sweeping the world.

The choice of the venue could not have been more pregnant with symbolism. For it was Germany in 1933 that marched to the drumbeat of right-wing Nazism. By 1945, that try-out had left 70 million people dead and a world devastated from Tokyo to Tallinn.

Seven decades later, the world again confronts the rise of Donald Trump in the United States, the consolidation of Vladimir Putin's power in Russia, the bizarre behaviour of Rodrigo Duterte in the Philippines and Recep Tayyip Erdogan's itch for absolute power in Turkey. This is now coupled with the alarming ascent of right-wing bigots in Europe complete with their anti-Muslim rhetoric, anti-immigrant walls, and an appeal to the basest instinct omniscient in the Westphalian construct a la nationalism.

These autocratic and intolerant Europeans include Geert Wilders of the Netherlands, Marine Le Pen in France, Viktor Orban of Hungary, and Jaroslaw Kaczynski of Poland - all making a serious bid for power. And India has already had its reactionary moment in May 2014. All this begs a fundamental question: Why has madness seized the world?

The answer is simple. Globalization has failed. The global economy and the global political order, colloquially called globalization, work for less than 1 per cent of the world's population. Today, just eight people in the world own as much wealth as half the human population does.

Out of the first 100 largest economies of the world, 69 are transnational corporations. For example, Walmart ranks 10th, way ahead of even many first-world countries. Their power, reach and influence shape the economic policies of numerous nations. It underpins the neo-liberal economic construct also known as the 'Washington consensus'.

Coupled with that is the spectre of more than 11 civil wars raging from west of the Indian border at Wagah right up to the Bosphorus Strait, which divides Asia from Europe before arcing downwards into Africa.

Most of these conflicts are the result of disastrous American interventionist policies in the Greater Middle East over the past 16 years that attempted to reshape the frozen geography of the region after the dismemberment of the Ottoman Empire in 1918. Other conflicts feed the voracious appetite of the military industrial complexes of the US and other European nations, including Russia. However, the blowback of these involvements has come in the form of millions of refugees swamping continental Europe.

All this has made people insecure and frightened, especially in open, liberal, and erstwhile inclusive democracies. When people are scared, they instinctively seek the safety of their home and hearth. They also shut their doors tight, batten down their hatches, and yearn for that strong person who can rid them of their fears. Identity and religion take centre stage as safety in numbers and veneration of the omnipotent man-god become the driving societal impulses.

However, this antidote does not work, as history has demonstrated time and again, for these 'man-gods' are, in fact, megalomaniac dictators who inevitably lead their people to disaster. Their strength is their biggest weakness. Power does not legitimize or humanize them; it corrupts and brutalizes them and their actions.

Never before has the need for alternate interpretations, convincing narratives, alternative economic models, and progressive political choices been more urgent than now. What then should be the core elements of this new construct?

The first element is re-interpretation of nationalism and patriotism. Today, they represent xenophobic tendencies based upon spawning terror of the 'other' and are exclusionary in character. What the world requires is a paradigm of progressive patriotism - a global movement that promotes inclusiveness.

The second element is to build an economy for the 99 per cent. Not a capitalist/socialist or a totalitarian economy, but a human economy that puts the human being at the centre of the economic project.

What does this mean in concrete terms? It does not mean jobs. It means sustainable livelihoods. For jobs are constructs of the industrial age. That era is ending, at least in manufacturing, where automation and robots are replacing human beings at an unimaginable pace. What is required is a return to the pre-industrial era, harnessing the power of the Internet, digitalization, analytics, and metadata to create models where people serve other people in a world that is increasingly flattening out, replacing horizontal hierarchies and feudal corporate and political oligarchies.

As the world heads towards 100 per cent digital connectivity, it is a new frontier of both innovation and ingenuity that has the potential to create evenly spread prosperity where everybody can have a slice of the pie. This also has the potential of mitigating, if not alleviating, the feeling of exclusion and insecurity that engulf vast majorities of populations in any given geography and is the fodder for jingoistic nationalism.

The third element is winding down conflicts that plague large parts of the world. The erosion of sovereignty because of the creation of transnational Facebook, Twitter, and Instagram give people the ability to connect with each other and build 'peace narratives' in contested geographies.

An interesting poser would be to make peace with terrorists - the likes of the ISIS, Taliban, Boko Haram, and Lashkar-e-Taiba. While that may not be feasible immediately, alternative narratives of peace and hope would certainly help in isolating these elements even in their own eminent domains.

Strong people's movements against governments and military complexes that benefit from the economics of war will also help. If a new vision is not crafted, the Pied Pipers of 2017 will only lead this world to an unmitigated disaster with catastrophic consequences, and India may just be pioneering this trend.

The Asian Age
18 March 2017

TRANSFORMING INDIA FROM A BALANCING TO LEADING POWER

A year ago, Indian Prime Minister Narendra Modi addressed a joint session of the US Congress, marking yet another new phase in the increasingly cooperative US-India relations. The address, on 8 June 2016, was the culmination of a process that began in 2005, when a New Framework for the India-US Defense Relationship was signed between President George W Bush and Prime Minister Manmohan Singh. Among a slew of deals forged under this framework was the Civil Nuclear Cooperation Initiative, a landmark agreement in Indo-American nuclear relations that marked a new understanding between the two nations on the issue of weapons of mass destruction.

Following the success of the Civil Nuclear Cooperation Initiative and the 123 Nuclear Agreement between the two countries, Congress introduced a bill in 2016 pertaining to defense and economic cooperation. This Special Global Partnership with India Act of 2016 promised to usher in a new level of Indo-US cooperation through large-scale transfers of technology as well as enhanced American military assistance to India.

However, much has changed at the White House since then, and questions regarding the Donald Trump administration's stance towards India abound. In the context of an increasingly assertive China and North Korea, this administration needs to continue to work to consolidate and enhance Indo-American relations to counter Chinese aggression. Furthermore, the White House should make clear in no uncertain terms that India is important in its own right, and not merely as a counterbalance to China.

During his campaign, President Trump indicated that

strengthening US-India ties would be a top priority for his administration. He went on to woo India by openly vilifying China on a host of issues not limited to the South China Sea. However, since he was sworn into office, Trump has displayed an unprecedented degree of warmth in his attitude towards China, leaving Indian observers puzzled. In his first few months in office, President Trump has demonstrated that Asia continues to be a major focus of the US foreign policy. His administration has addressed a multitude of issues related to China and the Korean Peninsula in a short time frame, reiterating US interests in the region. That being said, a more pressing concern is whether President Trump will work to enhance the stature of the Indo-American relationship in the same vein as his predecessors.

History

Upon attaining its independence in 1947, the newly formed Republic of India promptly inhabited a unique space in the global community of nations. On the one hand, its sheer size and geostrategic location made (and continue to make) it impossible for others to ignore it. Despite this, its post-colonial leaders opted to pursue policies of economic growth rather than develop indigenous military capacity. During the Cold War, Prime Minister Jawaharlal Nehru advocated the strategic policy of non-alignment – even though New Delhi did not want to develop the military means or the political wherewithal to actualize this concept.

Despite India's newfound focus on military growth, it is unlikely to take a hard shift towards the United States by rejecting this long-held policy of 'strategic autonomy,' which broadly resembles the Jeffersonian doctrine of avoiding the entanglement of formal alliances. However, the country may be amenable to quieter, subtler diplomacy. Thus, the United

States should instead consider an oblique strategy to finesse its relationship with India further.

Policy Shift

In March 2015, Foreign Secretary Subrahmanyam Jaishankar delivered a speech in which he declared that India was intent on playing the role of a 'leading' instead of a 'balancing' power in Asia. This purposeful announcement was predicated upon two decades of gradually increased presence, initiated by Prime Minister Atal Behari Vajpayee in 1998 and taken forward by Prime Minister Singh. While Vajpayee grabbed Washington's initial attention – and, indeed, the entire world took notice – by formally claiming nuclear status for his nation after its second successful nuclear test, signifying the beginning of India's endeavor at being a global power, Dr. Singh operationalized the newfound traction between the two countries by taking the relationship to a whole new level.

Since 2014, the National Democratic Alliance/Bharatiya Janata Party government has begun further consolidating strategic regional alliances, which would seem to indicate that it is perhaps countervailing perceived Chinese dominance in the region. Recent agreements with Mongolia, Sri Lanka and Bangladesh signify that India is looking to assert its position as a growing power. While these agreements may be either diplomatic or economic in nature, they appear to be a starting point for the current Indian government's attempt to offset Chinese ascendancy across the board.

Commonalities and Shared Interests

Several commonalities between the United States and India provide a genuine platform for cooperation. Primarily, both countries considerably value their political systems, which centre on democratic representation and liberal common values. The two countries have also suffered major terror attacks at the hands of Islamist terrorist groups, making the tackling of such factions around the world a priority on the Indo-American security agenda. India's economic growth lends further reason for enhanced cooperation, as the burgeoning marketplace yields several potential lucrative investment opportunities for the US government and American businesses and investors.

The two countries have seen eye to eye on their approach towards Beijing so far. Both nations realize the need to ensure that Beijing behaves in accordance with the rules of the liberal, postwar institutional order that the US helped build. As current and potential naval powers, the two countries must have unfettered access to international sea-lanes that Beijing intends to constrict. This leads to a broader, mutually beneficial reason for a coordinated policy towards China, a nation ostensibly not averse to flaunting a boosted militarism that could be dangerous to the security of both the US and India in the foreseeable future.

Chinese Presence in India's Backyard

The Indo-Chinese economic relationship represents an enigma to the United States. Despite the border and security-related tensions that have plagued the two nations, bilateral trade has continued to grow. Trade between India and China amounts to between $70-80 billion annually. To put that into context, trade between India and the United States has hovered between $100 and $110 billion for the past few years. An additional concern is that while India maintains a positive trade balance with the United States, it has had a significant trade deficit with China for over two years. China has invested heavily to establish its presence as an economic superpower across Asia, including in the Indian Ocean region – long seen as India's sphere of strategic influence. The recent Belt and Road Forum in Beijing sought to showcase the Belt and Road Initiative, including the strand called the China-Pakistan Economic Corridor, and is a manifestation of the changing geo-economic landscape of the region. China has signed contracts for development and operation of ports in both Pakistan and Sri Lanka, signifying its intent to expand its influence in South Asia. With these advances, the Chinese military footprint would extend from the periphery of India all the way to Guam.

An Old Friend Is Worth Two New Ones: Russia

Should India sense a lack of intent and purpose on the part of the United States, policy makers may instead turn to Moscow, which has developed a close relationship with Islamabad. This is underscored by the joint exercises undertaken by the Russian and Pakistani armed forces in the immediate aftermath of a lethal attack in September 2016 on an Indian military camp at Uri in Jammu and Kashmir, which resulted in significant casualties. In the immediate post-independence period, India put considerable effort towards developing close relations with the Soviet Union, driven by its socialist orientation at that time. Despite advocating nonalignment during the Cold War era, India often leaned towards the Soviet Union to counter the effect of the US-Pakistan relationship. New Delhi and Moscow have since worked closely on several endeavors. Moscow has served as India's preferred defense partner for a long time, signifying a level of historically established trust that has existed between the two nations.

While relations might not be as close today as they were a few decades ago, India and Russia continue to work together on several mutually important projects. They are associated through the BRICS alliance, which both countries have given importance to in the recent past. Despite quiet concerns in India about the life cycle costs of Russian-manufactured defense equipment, it continues to form a large part of India's arsenal, both aerially and navally. The two countries have shared a strong relationship historically. There is growing recognition of a gradual acceptance amongst policy elites in Washington that India will continue to maintain its relationship with Russia as well as China despite leaning closely towards the United States. For with the Chinese, the old adage applies: you cannot change your neighbours.

Need for Subtle Assistance

The United States must work with India to push back on the Chinese trajectory in certain domains. Policy makers and analysts warn that China is increasingly challenging American primacy in the 'command of commons'. There have already been significant disagreements between the US and China over issues such as the South China Sea, which poses a threat to American dominance in the global commons given that area's strategic significance.

Partnering with India could mutually benefit the United States and India in safeguarding global security, as well as in testing Chinese intentions in the region. The United States could assist India by providing the means to maintain its 'commanding position' in the Indian Ocean region. It is also essential for a growing India to now share responsibility for maintaining the global commons and to assert its jurisdiction over the Indian Ocean.

The current government is making the right noises about receptivity to foreign investment in the Indian defense sector.

There has already been some loosening up in Indian defense procurement processes and the United States should view it as an opportunity. President Trump, however, has not shown any indication of being likely to encourage arms sales to India. While Washington might not want to sell weapons to India, there are three areas – carrier aviation, space surveillance, and unmanned aerial vehicles – in which the United States could help India improve its capabilities in the sea, air, and space in the Indian Ocean region. Strengthening India in these three domains could help US military interests in the area, as India continues to maintain its preeminent position.

Carrier Aviation

India's military structure is based on carrier battle groups. Currently, the nation has only one aircraft carrier in its arsenal, the INS Vikramaditya, which it purchased from Russia. There are many observers in India and abroad who feel major purchases from Russia, including the carrier, could have been better handled. The INS Vikramaditya, previously named the Admiral Gorshkov, was delivered five years late and at triple the initially estimated cost, unsettling policy makers in New Delhi.

The Indian Navy has often neglected to develop certain essential naval assets such as submarines and anti-submarine helicopters – one reason for disproportionality between Indian and Chinese naval assets. China has two aircraft carriers currently in service and has displayed the ability to build more indigenously. Additionally, China has laid down plans that indicate it will be fielding two carrier strike groups in the Western Pacific Ocean and two in the Indian Ocean. This naval modernization push in the last decade has only widened the gap between the navies of the two countries.

India has realized its shortcomings in the recent past and has begun addressing these issues. A recently commissioned nuclear-capable submarine, the indigenously developed Arihant, is evidence of this paradigm shift. India also plans to deploy a second aircraft carrier, the INS Vikrant, by 2018. Despite these efforts, there will continue to be a mismatch between the naval forces of the two countries that India will struggle to balance on its own. The adoption of a long-term plan to enhance Indian naval capabilities would help mitigate this imbalance while presenting an opportunity for the United States as well.

Space Surveillance

Another area where cooperation can be elevated is in the domain of space surveillance. India and the US possess an impressive array of space assets. India's space programme has so far been largely concentrated on building civilian capabilities. As a result, military needs have often been neglected. Satellites are a key asset for the Indian military, as they are essential for monitoring Chinese military activities. Meanwhile, China has been increasing its own space-based capacity, including in navigation, intelligence, and communications assets, which give it a significant edge over India in the field. The United States should partner with India to improve space surveillance capacity. Cooperation between American and Indian surveillance assets could increase mutual Maritime Domain Awareness in the Indian Ocean region while simultaneously countering asymmetric Chinese space surveillance capabilities.

Unmanned Aerial Vehicles

Unmanned aerial vehicles (UAVs) are another aspect of the military that India has been looking to develop. Many of India's existing UAVs are either indigenously developed or

Israeli built. But the US can and should play an important role in this domain. There are proposals concerning the sale of the American developed drones to India, which operate at a greater altitude and possess further operational range than India's current fleet. India has focused on building effective drone capabilities that are important to the Indian military and can aid in surveillance of its borders. The difficult terrain of the region makes it challenging for other forms of surveillance and detection to be effective, making UAVs a preferred solution for the Indian Army. In addition to this, UAVs could be used to monitor China's military activities and military infrastructural development in the border areas. Drones provide an economically feasible solution to monitor the rapidly changing situation in border security. The Indian military is in the process of building a drone arsenal that is versatile in its functioning, and will continue to be a priority for them in the near future.

Possible Obstacles

It is vital for American interests in Asia to have India as an economic and strategic ally. However, for this relationship to work, President Trump will have to demonstrate his commitment to building a positive environment within which the Indian-American relationship can flourish. It is likely that the Indian policy making elite and body politic will expect President Trump to continue along the same path as his predecessors, and expect him to honour existing bilateral agreements. Furthermore, India would want the continuation of the recently signed nuclear agreements as well as the US-India Defense Technology and Trade Initiative, which the White House may review in the near future.

Importantly, President Trump has advocated several policies

that could harm Indian interests and potentially negatively affect the trajectory of US-India ties. To begin with, restrictions on work and education visas could antagonize India, with US-bound engineers set to suffer. Trump has also emphasized the need to bring processes back to the US that could cost Indian export of services heavily. With Indo-American trade already stagnating over the past few years, Trump's policies give no room for this trade to grow in the future. This will be a worrying factor for India. Environmental policy is another potential area of disagreement between the two countries. India has been a champion for renewable energy and has also shown a commitment to combating climate change, as is evident in its position on the Paris Agreement.

India has long appealed for the Kashmir issue to be solved bilaterally without international interference. Yet, in his statements, Trump has offered to mediate on the Kashmir dispute between India and Pakistan; New Delhi may not appreciate such involvement. Indian policy makers will be wary of Trump's policies towards Pakistan, and any decisions taken by the administration would go a long way towards determining the warmth of US-India relations. India would also want cooperation with the US on regional issues such as the Afghanistan conflict. Spillover from the destabilization in Afghanistan threatens to affect Indian security, which should be considered by the Trump administration before taking action in the country.

Conclusion

Given the advancements that China has made both economically and militarily, the US will need to channel considerable resources to assert its global and regional primacy. To accomplish this, India remains a key piece in the jigsaw for the United States. President Trump will need to assure India that it is not merely a regional prop to balance Beijing's power in the region, but a top priority for US foreign policy under the Trump administration. While Trump has favoured rapprochement with Beijing so far, more initiative and effort will be needed from Washington to ensure that the India-US relations continue to strengthen. The Asia-Pacific Stability Initiative proposed by Senator John McCain could be one effective way to signal the United States' intent towards India. The proposed $7.5 billion funding, if approved, could be a starting point for further India-US engagement in the years to come.

[co-authored with Bharath Gopalaswamy]

Atlantic Council

22 June 2017

IS OUR VIRTUAL WORLD MAKING US ALL ZOMBIES?

As I complete three years of my fortnightly tryst with this newspaper, I would like to focus on something completely apolitical. Let us discuss certain universal trends and what they tell us about the world that we live in. The first trend is the ubiquitous earphone or headphone. In any city or village, in India and abroad, you see both young and old with headphones thrust deep into their ears as they go about their daily lives.

Some of these contraptions are wired and others wireless, but the one thing that is common to these gizmos is the bubble in which their wearers live. In public spaces, metros, trams, airport lounges you have an entire bunch of people who are like zombies, either talking into those little microphones or laughing to themselves over a joke or an anecdote that resonates deep only in their ears.

No longer is there even a pretence of attempting to make polite conversation with the person next to you, and if you try to initiate small talk with someone who has these not-so-tiny buds sticking out of their ears, you are sure to be rewarded with a very exasperated and angry glare, which conveys in no uncertain terms the sentiment - buzz off, and mind your own business!

Now at one level, this may just be the right excuse for not interacting with strangers who you may never come across again in your entire life, but on an entirely different plane, it robs you of that 'chance conversation' that can both be meaningful and enlightening, if not life-changing. This bubble is actually stunting natural growth by enabling people to become absorbed in a virtual world that they create for themselves. It is like a gargantuan video game that each person plays with their own self, as they sleepwalk through life.

The skill of interacting with strangers, hearing their life stories, sharing their joys and disappointments, and being a part of the larger community of human beings is all but completely vanishing, as a whole new generation now believes that this insularity is the 'new normal'.

Coupled with this is the trend of customization. We now have the ability to customize what we read, see, and even do. This creates a vast echo chamber where we see what we want to see, hear what we want to hear, and read what we want to read. While on the surface this may seem perfectly normal and the ultimate panacea for interferences, it shuts out the alternative point of view, or the counternarrative.

There was a time when a newspaper gave you a cross-section of everything. Even if you did not want to read, let us say, the lifestyle section, it was still there. And as you flipped through a newspaper, something could possibly catch your eye and make you linger long enough to get you interested in something that wasn't your usual beaten track. Even with television, though you had the ability to flip through channels, you were not watching something that was always customized to your preferences.

However, now you have an entire generation that gets its information from their very own plate, be it the mobile screen, laptop screen or the 'smart' TV. It is like a made-to-order menu where your international news comes from a global broadcasting service, your domestic news from a particular newspaper, your sports feed from a specific sports website, and your weather update from a specialized weather forecasting service. All this would keep tumbling onto your Facebook homepage or any other home screen that you choose to create on your favourite electronic plate.

Coupled with that are the people you follow on Twitter or whom you choose to like on Facebook. Invariably, you do not follow or track those whom you do not like except if you are a troll, *bhakt*, or a pervert. This creates information skews, which penetrate the 'bubble' you have sought to enter.

I once had an amazing conversation with a brilliant young student of creative arts at a café in Washington D.C. He knew all the masters of painting, including the finer nuances of their works, and listening to him was like a tutorial on the history of painting, sculpture, and other forms of creativity.

However, he did not know that there was a war raging in Syria or for that matter what the ISIS stood for. He vaguely knew that there were some bad guys 'Islamists', as he had heard, who were killing people by driving big trucks into milling crowds. Beyond that he was not interested, for he thought that this was not a part of the 'beautiful echo chamber' that he had created around himself, and he just did not want to allow reality to intrude into his blissful and blessed existence.

However, it is extremely dangerous to grow up in a world where you customize your own reality by shutting everything else out. As the penetration of mobile phones, social media, and other such technologies grows, this 'echo chamber' would become all-pervasive and produce an entire generation of people who are intimately connected with themselves but disconnected from the reality around them.

They are always in a state of idyllic transcendental meditation. This could be good, but imagine an 11-year-old boy addicted to watching pornography on his mobile phone, either because his parents do not have the time to observe what he does online, or because they are sensitive about his privacy. Forget men and women, even kids do not share passwords of their phones and other such details with their parents.

The march of technology is fantastic, enabling you to hook up to a Wi-Fi network in a shopping mall and make a WhatsApp or a signal call to someone thousands of miles away, absolutely free of cost. On the flip side, this technology is creating walking, talking automatons whose comfort levels in their own surreal world may end up becoming an anathema to human civilization as we have known it.

The Asian Age
24 June 2017

US in a Post-Hegemonic World

WHY TRUMP RUBBISHED GOP LOYALTY OATH

Researching American constitutional law in connection with a legal preposition, I chanced upon the principled opposition of a distinguished lawyer, Denise Merrill, Secretary of State of Connecticut, who had been pressing for the repeal of a longstanding party loyalty law that allows party apparatchiks to expel a person from the party if s/he displays a lack of fidelity to the party's core principles. She argues that the party loyalty law is outdated and offensive to basic democratic principles. However, before examining that proposition, a fundamental question needs to be answered first. What are political parties? The United States Supreme Court examined this question with regard to the definition and character of political parties. In California Democratic Party vs Jones, 530 US 567 (2000), the US Supreme Court sought to distinguish between the private and public affairs of a political party: 'Representative democracy in any populous unit of governance is unimaginable without the ability of citizens to band together in promoting among the electorate candidates who espouse their political views. The formation of national political parties was almost concurrent with the formation of the Republic itself. Consistent with this tradition, the court has recognized that the First Amendment protects "the freedom to join together in furtherance of common political beliefs."'

However, the same US Supreme Court in the momentous matter of Elfbrandt vs Russell, in a 5 to 4 decision, declared unconstitutional Arizona's requirement of a loyalty oath from state employees. How does the loyalty question in the context of political parties play out in modern times? The last three remaining Republican nominees in the American presidential primaries perhaps gave the most prescient answer. When asked about the loyalty oath that they had signed to support the Republican nominee and not to run as an independent or as the candidate of another political party against him, Ohio governor John Kasich told CNN: 'All of us shouldn't even have answered that question.' Senator Ted Cruz went even further at a town hall saying, 'I'm not in the habit of supporting someone who attacks my wife and my family.' The moderator then asked Donald Trump whether he is sticking with his pledge to support the nominee. 'No, I don't anymore,' Mr Trump had said. 'No, we'll see who it is.' This was six months after all of them had signed a loyalty oath put out by the Republican Party in September 2015. It just goes to underscore the transient and fictitious nature of political loyalty vows.

In hindsight, it seems Mr Trump was far more in sync with the deep-seated resentment among the American people with the dysfunctionality of Washington D.C. and the incestuous nature of the US establishment. He did not want to be tied down to any commitment that would have precluded the option of running even as an independent. As events have by now testified, there was substantive silent support for Mr Trump that may have even put him as an independent candidate into the Oval Office in the event of the Republican Party deciding to dump him. It again reinforces the paradigm that politics has moved from being party-centric to individual-centric. With the advent of the new media that has made public discourse horizontal from vertical, the epitaph of the political party systems may truly be on the way to be written.

The march of history evidences that individuals have invariably been loftier than the political parties they represented. Winston Churchill was larger than the Conservative Party, Franklin D Roosevelt loomed over the Democrats, Indira Gandhi towered above the Congress Party, Zulfikar Ali Bhutto was heads and shoulders above the Pakistan People's Party and Margaret Thatcher soared over the Conservative Party. Even Narendra Modi is bigger than the BJP. With people now becoming weary of establishment politicians, this trend has intensified and Mr Trump is its latest manifestation. Loyalty oaths are best characterized as perverted litmus tests of paranoid states and organizations. During the period of McCarthyism in the US with its frenzy to root out Communists, the Weavers - an admired folk-singing quartet that consisted of Pete Seeger, Lee Hayes, Fred Hellerman and Ronnie Gilbert - were persecuted for refusing to sign a loyalty pledge. In Great Britain, an increasing number of MPs are refusing to swear allegiance to the British crown. Many have muttered uncharitable stuff about the archaic sovereign under their breath while reciting the pro-forma pledge only to be picked up by sensitive mikes and subsequently broadcast.

The incongruity of the fidelity paradigm was taken to an entirely different level in Nazi Germany. There, even the priests who were men of God were asked to swear allegiance to the Reich, thereby effectively putting the Nazi state even above God. Article 16 of the Reich Concordat of 1933 required Catholic bishops and priests to swear an oath of allegiance to the Third Reich. It read: 'Before bishops take possession of their dioceses they are to take an oath of fealty either to the Reich representative of the state concerned, or to the President of the Reich, according to the following formula: "Before God and on the Holy Gospels I swear and promise as becomes a bishop, loyalty to the German Reich and to the (regional) state of... I swear and promise to honour the legally constituted government and to cause the clergy of my diocese to honour it. In the performance of my spiritual office and in my solicitude for the welfare and the interests of the German Reich, I will endeavour to avoid all detrimental acts which might endanger it."'

That now brings us to India. Article 19 (1)(c) of the Constitution gives citizens the right to form associations and unions. Does that then necessarily entail that they can become closed structures that band together based on a shared set of doctrines and, therefore, have an inherent right to bar as member persons who do not demonstrate adherence to all the same dogmas? This was a proposition put forward in the BCCI vs Cricket Association of Bihar and others, while opposing the acceptance of the Lodha Committee recommendations. The proposition was rejected by the Supreme Court. Hypothetically, if it is argued that the above maxim is correct and the Supreme Court erred in striking it down, even then, can this be applied to political parties? Political parties are more than mere private voluntary organizations. They are public organizations. Since political parties are registered with the Election Commission in terms of Section 29A of the Representation of the People Act, 1951 and are subject to the rigours of Para 16A of the Election Symbols (Reservation and Allotment) Order, 1968, they stand on a different plane than non-government structures and must follow a different standard of public conduct.

It may not be constitutional or even legal to exclude from the ambit of a political party people who may not subscribe to each and every tenet and direction of a political party, for that would call into question both its inclusiveness and, more importantly, its representative character as a public organization. Too often loyalty oaths have been used to split people, to act punitively both retrospectively and prospectively towards those with whom there is a disagreement or whose influence is sought to be diminished if not eliminated. It is, therefore, conscientious to disagree with it from a purely philosophical, ideological, and legal postulate to loyalty oaths and affirmations. It is an idea whose time has expired. It is the leader in a person that people follow, not necessarily the political party.

The Asian Age
12 November 2017

WITH TRUMP IN CHARGE, WORLD FACES DILEMMAS

Donald Trump assumed office as America's 45th President on Friday. Over 25 years after the collapse of the erstwhile Soviet Empire in December 1991 and four Presidents in the interim period when the US regarded itself to be the only superpower in the world, the sheen today is off.

While any democratic nation is entitled to elect whosever they like, the one significant thing that Mr Trump's election underscores is the deep anxiety that Americans have about their future and what the complexities of the present world mean for the American way of life.

Immigration, the spectre of Islamic fundamentalism, and the loss of its manufacturing base essentially to China were the three hot-button issues that the politically correct establishment figures were unwilling to address. By taking these issues head-on early in the campaign, Mr Trump hit a raw nerve that resonated with the people, a reality that mainstream media in the US refused to acknowledge. That's all in the past.

Mr Trump has triumphed and now the show must begin in right earnest. What does the Trump presidency mean?

The first dilemma goes out to Southeast Asians - there is a perception that the Trump administration will not be as engaged in Southeast and even North Asia as earlier US administrations have been. In that event, a power vacuum will manifest, which China will be eager to fill. If the spectre of Chinese domination grows, where does that leave Australia, India, Japan, South Korea, and the littoral states of the South China Sea?

The second dilemma goes out to West Asians, or what is

referred to as the Middle East. As Mr Trump surveys the swathe of territory from the Strait of Bosphorus to the Khyber Pass and beyond that to the Wagah border between India and Pakistan, he sees a region in deep turmoil. The Trump administration has already sent out some strong signals about the way it would want to shape the Israel-Palestine conflict, and though the recent Paris Conference on this festering sore of history was largely factitious, it remains to be seen as to how the new administration looking at the region with a fresh pair of eyes can come up with workable policy prescriptions.

The third dilemma goes out to the ayatollahs of nuclear proliferation, arms-control regimes, and disarmament soothsayers. Mr Trump has tweeted for a qualitative and quantitative expansion of the US nuclear arsenal. There has always existed a minor school of thought in the US that more is better in terms of nukes. The question that it raises is: What would such a world look like? Would it spark off an arms race again with a resurgent Russia? Would it compel some of the yet undeclared nuclear weapon states to go public? This would have profound implications on international security that are too horrendous to even contemplate.

The fourth and final dilemma goes out to cyber-security mandarins. The recent presidential election in the US has challenged the fidelity of voting processes. The unanimous read of the intelligence boffins presented to Mr Trump pointed to alleged Russian interference in the US election processes. Does it have implications for other democracies around the world, especially in Europe, where a round of critical elections is coming up? These are some of the larger issues that are not country-specific.

India so far has been pretty nonchalant about the Trump presidency. There is a general belief that while Democrats are more feted by the Indian political elite, strategic thinkers believe that Republicans are better to do business with. In the past eight years of the Obama presidency, not a single big idea has either emerged or been conceptually incubated by the two countries. Would the Trump-India engagement be any different?

The concerns of the Trump administration over the need to rein in ISIS, withdrawal from the Trans-Pacific Partnership, the lack of a conceptual framework vis-à-vis the Afghanistan-Pakistan paradigm are some of the areas to which Indian policymakers must apply their minds. Does India fit into any of these concerns?

One of the frameworks that ostensibly attracts the new American administration is the size of the Indian defence establishment and its intrinsic institutional capacity. This in no way applies to the procurement potential that in any case has seen an exponential jump in the past few years. It, on the contrary, has everything to do with projecting power and putting it to practical use.

India was called upon by a previous Republican administration to weigh in when Iraq was invaded by a multinational coalition in March 2003. Even then, there was a BJP-led NDA government that was charged with the remit of steering the ship of the Indian state. However, Prime Minister Atal Behari Vajpayee wisely refrained from committing any Indian troops to that ill-advised venture. Would Prime Minister Narendra Modi respond differently if a similar call comes regarding the ISIS?

Mr Vajpayee is a liberal at heart; Mr Modi's core beliefs are closer to some of the ideologically-driven foreign policy positions that the Trump administration may decide to take. Coupled with the desire to stride on the global stage, ignoring the reality that India is home to the second-largest Muslim population that can proudly claim that none of them has ever been remotely allured by the medieval caliphate vision of the

ISIS, this government may inadvertently walk into a situation that can have domestic consequences as well.

The world of Mr Trump may be very different from what the world has so far encountered. It will, after the inauguration, have to constantly keep figuring out if the early morning tweets represent Mr Trump's personal views or carefully-crafted inter-agency-driven American positions articulated and executed in a calibrated manner. We surely do live in interesting times.

The Asian Age
21 January 2017

DYSFUNCTIONAL US FUELS GLOBAL ANXIETY

After a dizzying round of speaking engagements in Washington D.C., one can't but help come away with the impression that the capital of the United States is not only deeply divided but also mightily dysfunctional. The divide is not confined to the traditional Republican-vs-Democrat paradigm that has paralysed policy processes in that city for years, it now cuts across the Republican establishment itself. Perhaps for the first time it has also cleaved the deep state in the United States of America. On the streets, there are regular protests across American cities with the chant or the rant 'Not My President' slicing the frigid air.

Former Senate majority leaders Trent Lott and Tom Daschle of the Republican and Democratic parties respectively have written a brilliant book, *Crisis Point,* which maps the journey of the American Democratic experience and tries to suggest a fix to the broken politics in Washington and across America. However, the election of Donald Trump as President has only deepened these fissures. In America now a third category of politicos has come up, and they are called 'Trumpies' - the supporters and followers of Mr Trump.

Beyond the many wars that Mr Trump is fighting with the American media, the intelligence community and a host of world leaders - from Mexico to Australia - there is a sense of deep dread among the policy community that the Trump presidency may end up undermining the decades of hard work that has been done to establish America's global position.

What Mr Trump describes as the swamp that has to be drained

is an intricate web of lobbying firms, consulting companies and think tanks that cater to the power dynamics of a city whose influence extends much beyond its own beltway to the far corners of the world. What that swamp has also absorbed over a period of time is the best and the brightest brains in the US, limited not to the legal fraternity alone.

One of the greatest challenges the new administration faces is filling up thousands of vacancies that are coterminous with the term of any administration in the US. Given the fact that most of the 'bright sparks' in the Republican corner were signatories to a series of appeals that urged the American people not to vote for Mr Trump, they have been made persona non grata with the new administration. There was a window when Mr Trump and his core team were prepared to overlook the indiscretion, but after a row of spats with the mainstream media and the spook population, they have now circled the wagons.

If one was to go by the 'informed gossip' in the US capital, senior presidential adviser Steve Bannon is now the man in charge of the appointments processes and extreme ideological vetting is the order of the day. Since there is hardly any bench strength left on the Republican side, there is a desperate scramble to look beyond the talent pool and find people who were not signatories to various anti-Trump missives and are 'Trumpies' in some manner of speaking.

This means that quite a few positions in the US administration may remain unfilled for a while with the Obama holdovers continuing to run policy at the middle level.

Where does all this confusion leave India? Frankly, nowhere, because even after 40-odd days, there are no go-to people in Washington D.C. who are charged with the South Asia remit.

What then are the tea leaves that policymakers in New Delhi should read to determine the trajectory of the new US administration towards India, beyond the shenanigans of a bunch of carpetbaggers masquerading as Trump groupies, trying to peddle influence in New Delhi?

First and foremost, what will be the US policy towards Afghanistan? Gen. John Nicholson, the top American commander in Afghanistan, has asked for a surge of troops to deal with a resurgent Taliban. He told the Senate Armed Services Committee that enhanced troop numbers should come from both the US and its allies. He said: 'They could come from our allies as well as the United States. We have identified the requirement and the desire to advise below the corps level. It would enable us to thicken our advisory efforts across the Afghanistan mission.'

With US allies in no mood to step up to the plate, if Mr Trump heeds the general's request, he then needs to step back from the Jacksonian imperative that is running through the 'Trumpies', that the US must disengage from its global role. That in effect would also refix the policy towards Pakistan. More US troop numbers will mean more reliance and dependence on Pakistan. That automatically will translate into a re-hyphenation of India and Pakistan.

If the US would require Pakistani assistance in myriad forms in Afghanistan, then it obviously cannot and will not come down heavily on the terrorist infrastructure in that country, and therefore, the conventional American policy of paying lip service to Indian democracy while perpetuating an incestuous relationship with the Pakistani deep state will not only continue, but perhaps, intensify.

The second thing to watch out for is: What will be the US policy towards China? If Mr Trump is indeed serious about 'Make in America Again' and 'America First', then this should translate into reshoring of American manufacturing facilities. While automation and robotics will unfortunately ensure that this does not mean any substantive employment opportunities for the rust belt of the US, this will inject a new dynamic into the Sino-American equation.

If one was to look back to the July of 1971 when Henry Kissinger flew from Pakistan to Beijing to break the ice with Mao Zedong, it is American manufacturing that has substantively underpinned the Chinese economic miracle. As of 2015, the American investment in China was valued at $74.56 billion. The high point of the US-Chinese relationship was in 2009, when Barack Obama actually proposed a G-2 to handle global affairs after the economic meltdown.

If Mr Trump succeeds in luring even a fraction of that back or succeeds in stopping fresh American capital from being invested in China, it would introduce more than an element of strain into the relationship. This could work to India's advantage, not economically but strategically. From an economic perspective, 'America First' and NarendraModi's 'Make in India' are parallel tracks that are not destined to meet.

However, the fructification of this strategic lever for India depends upon another variable that is at the moment ambiguous. Would the US like to disengage from the Asia-Pacific? If Mr Trump's decision to renege on the Trans-Pacific Partnership is any indication, then in the coming months and years, a huge power vacuum is going to open up in the region. Each country will have to reevaluate and recalibrate its position over China. A lot of countries in the region may just decide to bend to the Chinese wind. In those circumstances, America's economic pullback from China will get replaced by investments and enhanced trade within the region. Strategically speaking, India will not be able to take any advantage of the likely US-China estrangement, for the Australia-India-Japan axis, without a US underpinning, will be like a car without wheels frozen in time and space.

For India, the best-case scenario will be American disengagement in Afghanistan enabling it to take a more objective position vis-à-vis Pakistan, coupled with a pullback on investments in China but continued engagement in the larger Asia-Pacific region. This will make a formal or non-formal quadrilateral of the US, Japan, India and Australia a reality. It will add to New Delhi's heft.

Finally, India has to watch out for the position that the Trump administration takes regarding the global trading order. It is amusing that the US now wants to demolish the multilateral trading system it so assiduously created over the decades and the President of the still totalitarian Communist state, the People's Republic of China, is the new poster boy of globalization. The paradox could not be droller. As of now, all the balls are in the air in Washington D.C., and India, like the rest of the world, is in a 'wait and watch' mode.

The Asian Age
4 March 2017

SPEAKING TRUTH TO POWER: DIFFERENT CHOICES

The President had identified his enemies by name but even the most powerful man in the world can only rant his frustration at the American press.

As I write from faraway Washington D.C., the contrast could not have been more stark. The press in the United States, almost without exception, is engaged in a rancorous battle with the current US administration, shining some light on it and speaking truth to power. Such is the exasperation of the White House that President Donald Trump took to Twitter on the morning of 6 June to launch a no-holds-barred diatribe against the media. He tweeted: 'The fake MSM is working so hard trying to get me not to use social media. They hate that I can get the honest and unfiltered message out.'

This tweet came a day after presidential aides tried to draw a distinction between the tweets labelling them as a social media phenomenon and government policy. Mr Trump undercut them the very next morning essentially saying that MY TWEETS MATTER. He went on to rub it in by directly hitting out at the most influential networks and print publications. He again tweeted: 'Sorry folks, but if I would have relied on fake news of CNN, NBC, ABC, CBS, washpost or nytimes I would have had zero chances of winning WH.'

Ironically, these tweets came on a day when 73 years ago Allied troops under the command of Gen. Dwight D. Eisenhower (later President) stormed the beaches of France, commencing the liberation of the European mainland. The flower of American youth fell to a barrage of German fire, but by sheer force of will they established a bridgehead. The battle for the beaches of Normandy, immortalised in the movie *The Longest Day*, was far from President Trump's mind when he tweeted a commemoration of that epoch-making struggle many hours after the media harangue.

The President had identified his enemies by name but even the most powerful man in the world can only rant his frustration at the American press and their unwillingness to play ball with him. He cannot set the Central Intelligence Agency, the Federal Bureau of Investigation or the Internal Revenue Service (IRS) and the various other law-enforcement agencies after them. For institutions in the American democratic paradigm are mature and robust, and they will not do the President's dirty work.

Mr Trump learnt it the hard way. His firing of FBI director James Comey has backfired on him so badly that the White House has been scrambling to do damage control and put out rapidly spreading bushfires that threaten to engulf those around him.

The story so far has been that President Trump ostensibly asked the FBI director to pull the plug on the investigation into Russian interference into the US presidential election process and the alleged meetings that the Trump campaign staff members had with senior Russian officials, including the Russian ambassador.

What the content of those meetings was, whether or not it was in any manner criminal in nature — would emerge as the investigation unfolds, but the rvelation that former national security adviser Michael Flynn was less than forthcoming about these Russian connections to vice-president Mike Pence has already cost him his job. Mr Comey's testimony on June 8 before the Senate Intelligence Committee could well become the trigger for the commencement of the impeachment of Mr Trump.

All this has come to a head in less than 150 days of the Trump presidency thanks to the relentless and dogged pursuit by the

American media which possibly is in the throes of its finest moment since the Watergate scandal. The American press is no babe in the woods. It is a corporate media, but it believes in the 'doctrine of institutional mistrust' that should underpin the relationship between the various stakeholders in a vibrant democracy. This is what I call the unkept media.

From the capital of capitals, when one turns one's gaze eastwards towards the world's most populous democracy – India – one is confronted with a bizarre spectacle where the government of Prime Minister Narendra Modi is brazenly throttling the freedom of speech and expression. The raids on NDTV and its promoters Prannoy Roy and Radhika Roy are nothing but a crude attempt to muzzle an alternative point of view that is troublesome to Modi and Co. by misusing the instrumentalities of the state – namely, the Central Bureau of Investigation, Enforcement Directorate and the Income Tax Department, to name a few.

The fact that a spurious case ostensibly relating to a banking transaction, that too with a private bank – which is not even a complainant in the matter – has been fabricated and deployed to unleash the 'might of the state' on the oldest and perhaps the most venerable English news channel only serves to underscore both the hubris and the insecurity of the NDA government. The fact that the CBI raids were perpetrated a few days after a BJP spokesperson was literally ordered off the channel by one of its most soft-spoken anchors for allegedly insinuating that the channel was running an agenda against the government is definitely not a coincidence.

However, what is most disappointing is the reaction of a large section of the Indian media. They chose not to cover, let alone protest against this atrocity by the state.

On the contrary, certain propaganda vehicles of the government masquerading as television news channels that

Arun Shourie has correctly characterised as 'North Korean television channels' and the government's bots and trolls on the social media were deployed to justify the crass actions of the state. Even the Editors Guild of India gave but a pro-forma statement that can be lamented for its tepidness, for it did not contain even a hint of temerity. The News Broadcasters Association, which holds itself out as the custodian of the freedom of the press and self-regulation in the broadcasting space, did not even have a pro-forma condemnation of the CBI raids on its website. A new phenomenon has emerged in the past 36 months in India – the spectre of the kept media.

Rather than speak truth to power, now you have 'kept television channels' and their associates in the print space falling over each other to justify, whitewash and even glorify every wrong of the government.

If the American media is basking in the glory of its finest hour, sections of the Indian media are sloshing around in their most ignominious moment.

Lal Krishna Advani, as the information and broadcasting minister of the Janata Party government from 1977 to 1980, famously remarked about the Indian press during the Emergency: 'You (journalists) were asked to bend, but you chose to crawl.' Today sections of the Indian media are behaving worse than that. For they are no longer fit to be termed as the press, but are unashamed propagandists of the government.

However, what this kept media does not realise and would do well to internalise the prophetic words of a German pastor, Martin Niemöller, immortalised on a plaque in the Holocaust museum in Jerusalem:

First they came for the Socialists, and I did not speak out
Because I was not a Socialist.

Then they came for the trade unionists, and I did not speak out
Because I was not a trade unionist.

Then they came for the Jews, and I did not speak out
Because I was not a Jew.

Then they came for me – and there was no one left to speak for me.

That is the intrinsic DNA of sycophants.

The Asian Age

10 June 2017

MODI-TRUMP MEETING: A ZERO-SUM GAME

In less than a week from now, Prime Minister Narendra Modi will travel to the US capital to call on a gentleman who, defying all odds, was sworn in as its 45th President on 20 January 2017.

The fact that Prime Minister Modi will be the 38th or perhaps 40th head of government/state to be fitted into Donald Trump's calendar may or may not be a reflection on the priority accorded to the Indian relationship. Even the prime minister of little Montenegro, Milo Djukanovic – the latest and 29th member of NATO – as well as Egyptian president Abdel Fattah el-Sisi, have beaten Modi to the gates of the White House.

Why the Indian carriage has not been getting any traction down the Washington D.C. beltway is not difficult to discern. For a start you have a very distracted President in Mr Trump. His incessant fracas with the US media, its Deep State (read *intelligence services*), the great Washington swamp of lobbyists, law firms and think tanks that have been around for at least a hundred years – and above all his inability to fill the myriad executive positions that fall vacant with the end of each Presidency – have hobbled Trump's administration even before it has completed its first 150 days.

It is to such a dysfunctional US capital that Modi is headed.

But beyond the skullduggery of domestic US politics there are deeper and more profound policy issues at play, where Indian and US interests deeply diverge – despite the polemical optimism of Modi's Indian-American supporters. These concern India's two close neighbours now lip-locked in a passionate economic and strategic embrace called the China Pakistan Economic

Corridor (CPEC).

If there is one relationship that President Trump is personally invested in, it is the tango with President Xi Jinping. This has nothing to do with India but has, at its core, a headache called the Democratic People's Republic of Korea, or North Korea.

The US has heavily invested, indeed is entrenched, in North Asia and South East Asia, since the end of the Second World War. From Japan to Singapore and beyond into Australia, a network of hub-and-spoke security alliances/military bases underpin the economic prosperity of this dynamic region. It also makes America the most influential hegemon and power balancer here.

This was the underlying reality of Barack Obama's famous but never-fully-fleshed out 'Pivot towards Asia' strategy. The truth today is that despite withdrawing from the Trans Pacific Partnership (TPP), the American girdle of economic and political alliances across the Pacific, even a maverick like Trump cannot just throw all these relationships overboard.

An enigmatic nation and its equally unfathomable leadership can upend this entire treaty structure intricately engineered over the past seven decades. North Korea has so far test fired 16 missiles this year alone while the US and allies like South Korea and Japan have helplessly looked on.

Trump understands that the only country that still has a hold over North Korea is China. Beijing can make this hermit nation change its behaviour, and that is why Trump went out of his way to woo President Xi, not forgetting to send a representative to the One Belt One Road (OBOR) conference last month in Bejing. Trump has publicly reneged on his commitment to designate China as a currency manipulator, a poll commitment he had repeatedly articulated on the stump.

Perhaps China could have been the one area of convergence between India and the US. After all both countries have a vested interest in ensuring that the Middle Kingdom doesn't threaten the power balance in Asia.

There is empirical evidence that buttresses that apprehension. First, China's rise has not been comforting. China has every intent of securing - by all manner fair and foul - the territorial advances it has made since 1949, both on land and at sea. What should worry all the seafaring nations, who have a stake in ensuring that sea-lanes of communication and commerce remain open, is China's inexorable trek towards the Indian Ocean.

The question Prime Minister Modi must ask himself on board Air India One is why the Chinese are driving towards the Indian Ocean and not upward to the North Pacific Ocean.

The answer stares the Indian policy wonks in the face. As of now 18 Chinese naval bases circumscribe the Indian Ocean in varying degrees of commissioning. This thrust southward is a track that will be minimally resisted by America, while simultaneously allowing for maximum consolidation of China's own influence through a creeping policy of strategic naval bases initially hidden as civilian maritime ports.

Remember that the Indian Ocean, as the name demonstrates, is India's traditional sphere of influence.

China has successfully hedged itself by not entering the regions where the big boys of the erstwhile Cold War play, namely in the Middle East and even the icy waters of the Arctic Ocean. Instead, it wants to know why the name of its new eminent domain, the Indian Ocean, is so sacrosanct.

Certainly this encirclement unequivocally threatens India as well as the US, given that the US remains the only country capable of projecting power much beyond its shores.

But the sad truth is that in the current state of courtship between the US and China, Modi will find no takers even if he elects to raise India's concerns about Beijing.

The other invisible 600-pound gorilla in the Indo-US relationship is Afghanistan. After 16 years of continuous US presence, which has cost billions of dollars and hundreds of American lives, the current administration like the previous one, is desperately looking for a way out.

There isn't one. Except, perhaps, an ignominious exit that may put the country back in the hands of Pakistan-backed terror groups, ranging from the Haqqani network to the Quetta/Peshawar Shura, and of course the notorious Taliban. This gives Pakistan back the strategic depth it desperately craves for since the beginning of the current phase of US involvement and leaves the US exactly where it was 16 years ago. Meanwhile, Afghanistan threatens to return to instability and become an ungoverned and ungovernable space that can provide safe harbour to Islamists and terrorist groups of every shade and hue.

The US commander in Afghanistan, Gen. Nicholson and US Defence secretary James Mattis have told the US Congress that the US is not winning in Afghanistan; that the war is stalemated. There is no clarity either in the Pentagon or National Security Council as to the core US security interest in Afghanistan. Is it defeating the Al Qaeda, ISIS, Taliban or stabilizing the tottering Afghan state? All of them, any of them or none of them?

In the absence of any clear objectives, US policy today is in a splendid state of suspended animation. On the one hand there is the proposal to add another 5000 US troops (euphemistically labelled trainers), although it remains unclear why a multinational force consisting of more than a 100,000 troops and backed by close air support, drones and other gizmos, hasn't been able to defeat the Afghan bigots over the years.

The other option currently in vogue in the US capital is to sup with the devil i.e. raise the ghost of ISIS presence in Afghanistan, and use it as a pretext to cut a deal with the Taliban.

In each of these scenarios India does not figure or fit in. An American surge, however limited, only increases US logistical dependence on Pakistan. If the Taliban have to be mollycoddled, then Pakistan's ISI becomes the interlocutor of compulsion, for they are the ones who have sustained the Taliban over the past two decades, while ingesting billions of American dollars to ostensibly defang them.

India has no grand strategy that underpins its foreign policy nor much resonance left in world capitals. Holy cows, mythical properties of their pungent nectar, the brutal lynching of minorities and ruthless suppression of media freedoms are the only news out of India in the Western media these days.

It can be safely wagered that except for grandiloquent pronouncements and more taxpayer's money squandered on gratuitous defense procurement, nothing will come out of Modi's visit to America. If at all, India will be reduced to a sponge for the US military-industrial complex rather than become an equal partner or its respected strategic ally.

The Indian Express
21 June 2017

Part II

The Institutional Challenge

AN INJUDICIOUS DELAY

The Chief Justice of India twice - on August 12 and again on August 15 - expressed his anguish over the obduracy of the NDA government for sitting on the recommendations made by the Supreme Court collegium for the appointment of judges to various High Courts across the country.

Earlier, in April 2015, there were painful photographs in the media of a visibly perturbed Chief Justice TS Thakur articulating his torment over the obstinacy and foot dragging on judicial appointments by the government directly to the Prime Minister.

The fact that the CJI had to upbraid the government and caution them not to compel the Supreme Court to pass judicial orders for the appointment of judges is a telling comment on the unfortunate gridlock created by the executive in the administration of justice.

Justice TS Thakur's decision to take judicial notice of the paralysis in the appointment process should not be taken lightly. In a country of 1.3 billion people, with crores of cases pending in various courts at every level, it is hardly conducive to filling the vacancies in the High Courts averaging 45 per cent. On the one hand, Prime Minister Narendra Modi sanctimoniously harangues judges to take fewer vacations but on the other hand, his government has no compunctions about delaying critical judicial appointments.

This government's major objective has been to execute a hostile takeover of the judicial appointment process.

In one of its first actions, the NDA derailed the recommendation for the appointment of an eminent senior counsel to the Supreme Court. It is alleged that the 'powers that be' were unhappy with him as he was an amicus curiae in the Gujarat fake encounter cases that took place when Mr Modi was chief minister and BJP president Amit Shah was the state home minister. Some of the encounters were admitted as fake by the Gujarat government on an affidavit before the Supreme Court and even interim compensation was paid to the next of kin even before the matter was formally adjudicated by the court and appropriate directions given and orders passed.

This was followed by the constitutional amendment to introduce the National Judicial Appointments Commission. After a marathon hearing, a Constitution Bench of the Supreme Court rightly struck down the amendment and reverted to the collegium system of judicial appointments in October 2015. Since then, appointments have come to a standstill. In fact, the process of appointment to the High Courts has been deadlocked for almost two years now.

As per the vacancy positions released by the ministry of law and justice on 1 August, out of the total sanctioned strength of 1,079 judges in all the High Courts, the current working strength is 601. After the Chief Justice of Bombay High Court retired on August 10, the working strength is down to 600, marginally above 55 per cent of the sanctioned strength.

High Court	No. of Judges	
	Current	Sanctioned
Chhattisgarh	8	22
Karnataka	26	62
A.P. & Telangana	24	61
Madras	38	75
Allahabad	78	160
Patna	27	53

The above statistics is only illustrative of the working situation in different High Courts and the judges' burden with a colossal daily inflow of matters. The figures highlight the primary reason for unusual delays in disposal of cases and the rise in the pendency.

It's no rocket science to discern that the government wants to have a say in the appointment process, presumably with a view to indulging in 'court packing' and appoint judges whose ideology is compatible with the Sangh Parivar's. This would be catastrophic to say the least. The government is the country's largest litigant, and if judges were to toe the ideological line of the government or the ubiquitous Sangh Parivar then justice would be an elusive concept.

Since 2014, the judiciary has struck down the National Tax Tribunal Act, the NJAC Act and the 99th Constitutional Amendment, and the proclamation of President's Rule in Uttarakhand and Arunachal Pradesh – decisions that the Narendra Modi government finds difficult to stomach. The question that comes to mind is: Could the rule of law have been upheld if the judiciary was under government control?

What's more alarming, however, is the manner in which the government is attempting to override the Supreme Court judgment on NJAC and muscle into judicial appointments through the memorandum of procedure, by seeking to relegate the seniority clause of the judges of the High Courts in the appointment to the Supreme Court.

The minister of law and justice gave the game away when he bull-horned that Mr Modi, being a constitutional authority, must have a say in the appointments. It underscores the malevolent mindset of the present dispensation.

The government is sitting on two recommendations for the transfer of judges of High Courts, even as more than 200 recommendations are pending consideration, thereby precipitating a flashpoint between the judiciary and the executive. It is preposterous for the government to induce this paralysis, for after all, the sufferer is the small litigant who has to wait in queue for years to get small disputes adjudicated.

The situation of undertrials is also extremely disturbing and there is an urgent need to deal with the many criminal cases that cause people to languish in jail for years on end, in clear disregard to the due process of personal liberty enshrined in the Constitution. Justice must not only be done, but seen to be done, and if the government does not change its attitude towards appointments to the High Courts, and continues to sit on the recommendations made by the collegium, justice will elude many.

The one thing Mr Modi has not come to terms with is that the executive is just one of the stakeholders in India's power paradigm. As Lord Acton famously said: 'Power tends to corrupt, and absolute power corrupts absolutely.' This seems to be the only reason why the prime minister and his minions are trying to stare the judiciary down. There is a great peril that stalks this ancient land.

The Asian Age
20 August 2016

SC RULING ON RELIGIOUS APPEAL FOR VOTES WILL CLEANSE POLITY

The Supreme Court of India on 2 January 2017 delivered a pathbreaking judgment. If properly implemented, it would redefine the very essence of politics in India. Before venturing into an analysis of the implications of the said judgment, it would be appropriate to lay out the facts briefly.

The entire lis was predicated on the interpretation of the word 'his' in Section 123(3) of the Representation of People Act, 1951.

Justice Chandrachud explained it beautifully in the opening para of his dissenting judgment:

'This reference to a Bench of seven Judges turns upon the meaning of a simple pronoun: "his" in Section 123(3) of the Representation of the People Act, 1951. A word, it is said, defines a universe. Words symbolize the human effort to contain the infinity, which dwells in human relationships into finite boundaries, which distinguish the known from the unknown, the familiar from the unfamiliar and the certain from the uncertain. That so much should turn upon the meaning, which we assign to a single word, is reason enough to guard against an assumption that the issue that we confront is a matter entirely of grammar or of statutory interpretation. Underlying the surface of this case, are profound questions about the course of democracy in our country and the role of religion, race, caste, community and language in political discourse. Each of these traits or characteristics defines identity within the conception of nationhood and citizenship. Quibbles over the meaning of a word apart, the interpretation that will be adopted by the court will define the boundaries between electoral politics on the one hand and individual or collective features grounded in religion, race, caste, community and language on the other.'

Section 123 was amended in 1961 and the words 'systematic appeal' to vote in the name of religion, race, caste or community was deleted to widen the amplitude but the inclusion of 'his' religion, race, caste, community or language created confusion.

Referring the matter to a bench of seven judges, a constitution bench of five judges delineated the controversy as follows in their order dated 30 January 2014:

'As it appears, under the amended provision, the words "systematic appeal" in the pre-amended provision were given a go-by and necessarily therefore the scope has been widened but by introducing the word "his" and the interpretation given to the aforesaid provision in the judgments referred earlier, would give it a restrictive meaning. In other words, while under the pre-amended provision it would be a corrupt practice, if appealed by the candidate, or his agent or any other person to vote or refrain from voting on the grounds of caste, race, community or religion, it would not be so under the amended provision so long as the candidate does not appeal to the voters on the ground of his religion even though he appealed to the voters on the ground of religion of voters. In view of certain observations made in the Constitution Bench decision of this Court in Kultar Singh Case we think it appropriate to refer the matter to a larger Bench of seven Judges to consider the matter.'

The minority judgment delivered by Justices Goel, Lalit, and Chandrachud held 'that the expression "his" in Section 123(3) must mean the religion, race, community or language of the candidate in whose favour an appeal to cast a vote is made or that of another candidate against whom there is an appeal to refrain from voting on the ground of the religion, race, caste, community or language of that candidate'.

However, the majority judgment authored by Justices Madan Lokur and Nageshwar Rao and supported by the opinions of Justice

Bobde and Chief Justice (now retired) Tirath Singh Thakur gave Section 123 (3) a more expansive meaning. In their order, Justices Lokur and Nageshwar Rao held as follows:

'...for maintaining the purity of the electoral process and not vitiating it, sub-section (3) of Section 123 of the Representation of the People Act, 1951 must be given a broad and purposive interpretation thereby bringing within the sweep of a corrupt practice any appeal made to an elector by a candidate or his agent or by any other person with the consent of a candidate or his election agent to vote or refrain from voting for the furtherance of the prospects of the election of that candidate or for prejudicially affecting the election of any candidate on the ground of the religion, race, caste, community or language of (i) any candidate or (ii) his agent or (iii) any other person making the appeal with the consent of the candidate or (iv) the elector.'

Shorn of legalese, what it means is that religion cannot be invoked in elections for the purposes of getting votes whether the religion is of the candidate, his election agent, any person acting on his behalf or even the religion of the elector.

With one sweep, the Apex court has reiterated the founding values of the Indian Constitution – the complete separation of the church and the state. What it means is that religion is a purely personal affair in the private domain. While every person has the right to preach, practise, and propagate his or her faith, it has no place in the public affairs of the nation. This judgment would redefine the Indian polity and cleanse it of all the aberrations that have crept into the electoral arena since the first general elections in 1952. It would spell the death knell of identity politics and rightly so.

The Economic Times

1 January 2017

WILL THE 'BASIC STRUCTURE' BE THE NATION'S SAVIOUR?

Earlier this week was the 44th anniversary of the most seminal event in Indian jurisprudence. On 24 April 1973, the 'basic structure doctrine' of the Indian Constitution was midwifed into life by the largest-ever bench of the Supreme Court of India to be constituted till date.

A doctrine was conceptualised by the Supreme Court of India to circumscribe the amending powers of Parliament with regards to certain articles of the Constitution which were held to be the core or basic structures of India's founding document.

A bench of 13 judges of the Supreme Court by a majority of seven judges to six, decided that the Constitution could not be amended in a manner that distorted its basic structure. Intriguingly, 12 of the 13 judges didn't say a word about the 'basic structure' in their pronouncements. While six ruled that there were implied limitations on the amending power of Article 368 of the Constitution, and the other six held that the power was unlimited. The law of the basic structure came from the pen of one judge, Hans Raj Khanna, and this was adopted by the court through a judicial order entitled 'View of the Majority', a document in the form of an order of the court signed only by nine judges out of 13 on the bench.

An unfortunate fallout of the judgment was the supersession of Justices Amar Nath Grover, Jayanti Manilal Shelat and Kawdoor Sadananda Hegde because they had batted on the side of the basic structure. AN Ray, who was fourth in the order of seniority, was made the Chief Justice of India.

The question of the legitimacy of the basic structure

doctrine was raised immediately thereafter, and critics refused to recognise the order signed only by nine of the 13 judges to be the law laid down by the court.

By a quirk of fate the doctrine got further legitimacy after the Allahabad High Court set aside the election of Prime Minister Indira Gandhi and the then government amended the Constitution to introduce the 39th Amendment, by which the election of the Prime Minister and some other high dignitaries could not be called into question before a court of law.

When the amendment was challenged before the Supreme Court on the ground that it violated the basic structure of the Constitution, the then Attorney General conceded the doctrine. The amendment was struck down on the basis of the basic structure doctrine. Soon thereafter, an aborted attempt was made to review the basic structure doctrine but after two days the review bench, again of 13 judges, was dissolved abruptly, never to reconvene. Thus, the basic structure doctrine got consecrated as the holy grail of jurisprudence.

One can only wonder what would have happened if the Attorney General had not conceded the doctrine, but challenged its very existence during the 39th Amendment to the Constitution, specially since the entire court at that point had only one judge who had subscribed to the doctrine, namely Justice Khanna.

To get over the bar of the Kesvananda Bharati judgment, the 42nd Amendment was enacted into law by Parliament in 1976. It added to the amending power of Article 368 of the Constitution Clause 5, which reads: 'For the removal of doubts, it is hereby declared that there shall be no limitation whatever on the constituent power of Parliament to amend by way of addition, variation or repeal the provisions of the Constitution under this article.' Evidently, the language employed by the draftsman of this clause had a single agenda – to declare that the power of Parliament to amend the Constitution was unlimited and unfettered.

Since its discovery by Justice Khanna's pen, the 'basic structure' doctrine has been employed five times to strike constitutional amendments down – the 39th Amendment tailored to insulate the Prime Minister's and other high constitutional dignitaries' elections from legal challenge, the refusal to the vital right of judicial review in the cases of Minerva Mills, Kihoto Hollohan and L. Chandra Kumar. More recently, the court struck down what is popularly referred to as the National Judicial Commission Amendment because it fell foul of the independence of the judiciary, a basic feature of the Constitution.

What started as a struggle between the court and the government on property rights expanded into a battle for the soul of the Constitution. It became a confrontation between the judiciary and the legislature that the Constitution should not be so altered that it loses its fundamental identity.

The Kesvananda Bharati case happened at a point in time when many of the eminences in the current Union government were apprehensive of India becoming a one-party state – a fear that turned out to be unfounded. However, in a reversal of fortune the spectre of totalitarianism, fear of intolerance and India morphing into a one-party state looms large over this country from the very ones for whom Kesvananda Bharati had come as a sigh of relief in 1973.

As institutions are openly being subverted from within and without, as fundamental freedoms of thought, expression, worship are sought to be bludgeoned into conformity, as culinary choices are now the staple of lynching, mobocracy and vigilantism, as substantial sections of the so-called free media are behaving like pet performing poodles of the rulers and as even the legitimacy of democratic outcomes is the subject matter of substantive scepticism, if not outright derision, one cannot help but salute those nine wise men, specially Chief Justice Sikri, who devised the instrument of the order of the majority and breathed life into a Constitutional fiat called basic structure. Should we say – may God bless them? It may just be the only safeguard left to protect, preserve and uphold the founding vision of India if the Opposition does a humpty-dumpty on the nation.

The Asian Age
29 April 2017

FACED WITH TYRANNY, INDIA NEEDS AN ACTIVIST PRESIDENT, NOT A CONFORMIST

The President of India occupies a peculiar position in the Indian Constitution. On paper he is vested with a lot of authority, but in reality he is supposed to be a mere rubber stamp who endorses and thus legitimises every decision of the executive, however illegitimate it may be. Unlike the Governor, who has the powers to recommend the dismissal of a state government, the President doesn't have the same authority in relation to the Union government.

Article 53 of the Constitution vests in the President the executive power of the Union as also the Supreme Command of the Defence Forces. The phraseology of the Article, however, puts the Presidency seemingly on a tight leash as exemplified by the construct of the second proviso of this Article that states, 'Without prejudice to the generality of the foregoing provision, the Supreme Command of the Defence Forces of the Union shall be vested in the President and the exercise thereof shall be regulated by law.'

In fact the President may well ask the question: What is this law which circumscribes the untrammelled exercise of the Supreme Command of the Indian Defence establishment?

Article 74 (1) of the Constitution, which further titularises the Presidency, goes into the nub of this power conundrum: 'There shall be a Council of Ministers with the Prime Minister at the head to aid and advise the President who shall, in the exercise of his functions, act in accordance with such advice. Provided that the President may require the Council of Ministers to reconsider such advice, either generally or otherwise, the President shall act in accordance with the advice tendered after such reconsideration.'

Thus the rites of passage of emasculation of the Presidency seem to be truly consecrated in concrete.

However, a crucially important distinction is contained in the subtle wording of Article 60, which details the Oath or Affirmation that must be sworn by the President before s/he enters office. This includes the key phrase, '... (I) will to the best of my ability preserve, protect and defend the Constitution and the law...'

This is what sets the Presidency apart. All other constitutional functionaries, including the Vice President, the Prime Minister and even the Chief Justice and/or the Comptroller and Auditor General of India swear an oath that obliges them to 'bear true faith and allegiance to the Constitution of India as by law established.'

It's clear that in our constitutional scheme of things, the principal preserver, protector and defender of the Constitution is the President, not the Chief Justice of India and much less the Prime Minister. The President is constitutionally mandated and empowered to be the first responder in case there is an assault or even an insult to the Constitutional fabric. It therefore automatically flows from the above that the Presidency can well go beyond the boundaries of both Article 53 (2) and 74 (1) if it envisages that a constitutional transgression is being perpetrated.

Therein lies the opportunity for the parliamentary Opposition to find a candidate who is well versed in these constitutional subtleties, and not diffident about using these constitutional prerogatives if push comes to shove.

That's why the chosen one must spend the campaign period,

say from 16 June to 16 July, travelling across the country and articulating and expounding upon his perception of the role and responsibility of the Presidency, as propounded by the founding fathers in the Constitution and succinctly encapsulated in its Preamble.

The reason why this Presidential bulwark is more important than ever before is because the current NDA/BJP government does not believe in either the founding vision of India, fundamental freedoms guaranteed by Part III of the Constitution and other constitutional guarantees, including the rule of law essential for the basic functioning of any civilized nation.

The last three years bear eloquent testimony to the repeated, brutal and sustained assaults on the freedom to think, express, eat, wear clothes of your choice or even enjoy the liberty of India's public spaces. The conception of a public space that catalyzes original and creative thinking, celebrates dissent and respects an alternative viewpoint, howsoever virulent it may be, is anathema to this government.

Public lynchings in the name of the cow and the new Prevention of Cruelty to Animals (Regulation of Livestock Markets) Rules, 2017, notified by the government on its third anniversary, are all designed not to protect bulls, bullocks, cows, buffaloes, steers, heifers, calves and camels, but to emphasize the otherness of people.

In an atmosphere of fear and trepidation when tyranny permeates the hot summer winds, India does not require a conformist President, it requires an activist one. It does not require a copybook President, it requires a President whose only book is the Constitution of India. Copybooks were unable to prevent the unconstitutional overthrow of democratically elected governments in Arunachal Pradesh and Uttrakhand run by Opposition parties; neither they prevented the subversion of the democratic mandate in Goa and Manipur, nor pushed back on the orchestrated and calibrated attempt to disband the Republic of India and create a theocratic oligarchy.

That is why the Opposition cannot and must not agree to a President by consensus. A consensus is always a subscription to conformism. A contest, on the other hand, would allow the joint opposition the opportunity to once again lay before the people the Constitutional vision of India, in sharp relief to the paranoid jingoism of majoritarianism that we have today.

It would also unroll the philosophical stencil for the 2019 generale election.

As for candidates the Opposition should look at, beyond political players, at people who have experience in defending the Constitution. These include retired chief justices like Manepalli Narayana Rao Venkatachaliah, Tirath Singh Thakur, Justices AP Shah and Santosh Hegde, the eminent jurist Fali Nariman or the gentleman who is a close witness to the evolution of India, Dr Karan Singh. The litmus test of such a candidate must be 'who' can push the Constitutional envelope beyond the current pale to protect and defend it.

The Indian Express
30 May 2017

ANSARI SHOULD HAVE SPOKEN OUT WHEN MD. AKHLAQ WAS LYNCHED

Article 60 of the Constitution lays down the oath to be sworn by the President before entering office. What is vital in this oath are the words 'preserve, protect and defend the Constitution and the law'. The oath of the Vice President contained in Article 69 is virtually analogous. Article 65 further states that in the event of the occurrence of any vacancy in the office of the President, the Vice President shall act as President until the date on which a new President is elected.

Though the Vice President is also Chairperson of the Council of States and theoretically is but a heartbeat away from the presidency, in real terms it means nothing. Both the President and the Vice President are but mere symbols of the state rather than its pillars. Nonetheless, both the President and the Vice President have a constitutional and moral obligation to preserve, protect and defend the Constitution. That provides the constitutional leeway to step beyond the straitjacketed confines of their ceremonial existence. However, the timing of their actions or interventions is of the essence.

Profound differences

The first President of India, Rajendra Prasad, differed with Prime Minister Jawaharlal Nehru on the Hindu Code Bill. Prasad wrote to Nehru on 15 September 1951: 'My right to examine it (the Bill) on its merits, when it is passed by the Parliament, before giving assent to it is there. But if any action of mine at a later stage is likely to cause embarrassment to the Government, I may take such appropriate actions as I may be called upon to avoid such embarrassment consistently with the dictates of my own conscience.' This was before the Bill was even formally presented to Parliament by the government.

Giani Zail Singh had profound differences with Prime Minister Rajiv Gandhi. He refused to sign the contentious Indian Post Office (Amendment) Bill, 1986, that would have empowered the government to censor personal mail; sought the government's reason for not embracing a clear policy on the appointment of Supreme Court and High Court judges; queried the government's media coverage policy... the list goes on and on. Was he right on doing so? Perhaps not. However, he did not wait for the end of his term to articulate his opinion. President KR Narayanan repeatedly wrote rather tough missives to Prime Minister AB Vajpayee between 28 February and 15 March 2002, calling for an explanation on why the NDA/BJP governments failed to pre-empt, prevent and then stop the Gujarat pogrom. It is sad the Delhi High Court blocked the release of those critical letters even 10 years later in 2012.

Timing is of essence

In that context, the track records of the previous presidency and vice presidency are perhaps blotted. The President could have stayed his hand on the promulgation of President's Rule in Uttarakhand, stepped in when sequential constitutional coups were being carried out in Arunachal Pradesh. Similarly, the Vice President should have spoken out when Mohammad Akhlaq was lynched [in 2015] for allegedly possessing beef. He should have gone for his burial. It would have sent a salutary message to both the government and the community, for that is the inflection point that made Muslims insecure.

Delivering homilies at the end of the term can end up being

critiqued as a case of sour grapes or a parting kick. Does it bestow glory on high constitutional offices? The jury is out on that.

The Hindu
18 August 2017

Quest for Free Speech

FREE SPEECH LAWS MUST BE MADE STRONGER

'Unlike the US, the Indian Constitution does not guarantee the freedom of the press.' An invitation to be a part of a panel in Bengaluru on draconian laws in the context of freedom of the press – namely sedition, defamation, contempt and privileges – once again provided an opportunity to revisit the conundrum as to how free is free speech in India for both the media and the people.

Interestingly, unlike the United States and many other Constitutions around the world, the Indian Constitution does not guarantee the freedom of the press. It is a derivative of the right to freedom of speech read into the scope of this fundamental right available to citizens through judicial pronouncements. The question therefore still remains open: are media entities citizens within the meaning of Article 19(1)(a) of the Constitution of India.

The cornerstone of free speech in India is this article. The original article as adopted by the Constituent Assembly stated: 'All citizens shall have the right to freedom of speech and expression. The un-amended Clause 2 of this article that curtailed and circumscribed this freedom as adopted by the Constituent Assembly read as follows: Nothing in sub-clause (a) of clause (1) shall affect the operation of any existing law in so far as it relates to, or prevents the State from making any law relating to, libel, slander, defamation, contempt of court or any matter which offends against decency or morality or which undermines the security of, or tends to overthrow, the State.'

The scope of the restrictions was very wide in their amplitude even in their first conception. It allowed the State to make laws to deal with transgressions of seven different aspects of free speech. Notwithstanding this heft of restrictions, the assault on the freedom of speech and expression commenced in the very nascent years of the Indian Republic. On 10 May 1951 the statement of objects and reasons of the very first Constitution Amendment Bill had this to say about Article 19: 'During the last 15 months of the working of the Constitution, certain difficulties have been brought to light by judicial decisions and pronouncements, specially in regard to the chapter on fundamental rights. The citizen's right to freedom of speech and expression guaranteed by Article 19(1)(a) has been held by some courts to be so comprehensive as not to render a person 43 culpable even if he advocates murder and other crimes of violence. In other countries with written Constitutions, freedom of speech and of the press is not regarded as debarring the State from punishing or preventing abuse of this freedom...'

The first amendment, therefore, proceeded to enhance the restrictions in Clause 2 of Article 19. After the amendment, it now reads: 'Nothing in sub-clause (a) of clause (1) shall affect the operation of any existing law, or prevent the State from making any law, in so far as such law imposes reasonable restrictions on the exercise of the right conferred by the said sub-clause in the interests of the security of the State, friendly relations with foreign states, public order, decency or morality, or in relation to contempt of court, defamation or incitement to an offence.' The addition of the words 'reasonable restrictions on the exercise of this right' enabled the Supreme Court to uphold the colonial relic – the prince of oppression Section 124A of the

Indian Penal Code – the Law on Sedition.

After the Constitution came into force, it was widely expected that this section of the IPC would become violative of the fundamental right to freedom of speech and expression. Thus sedition, a draconian law of the colonial era, would have been out of the penal code for good.

However, this did not happen because in 1962 the Supreme Court on the strength of the first Constitutional Amendment upheld the constitutional validity of Section 124A in Kedarnath Singh vs State of Bihar (AIR 1962 SC 955). During the colonial period, sedition was considered a black law and was used extensively against the leaders of the freedom movement. Gandhi, Tilak and many other leaders were put behind bars for many years under this law. But a Constitution Bench of the Supreme Court upheld its vires and presented it before free India as a necessary virtue in the interest of the survival of republic.

Again in 1963, the freedom of speech and expression was further assaulted with the addition of the words 'sovereignty and integrity' of India. The statement of objects and reasons of this particular amendment outlining the reasons for this insertion were: 'The Committee on National Integration and Regionalism appointed by the National Integration Council recommended that Article 19 of the Constitution be so amended that adequate powers become available for the preservation and maintenance of the integrity, and sovereignty of the Union. The committee were further of the view that every candidate for the membership of a State Legislature or Parliament, and every aspirant to, and incumbent of, public office should pledge himself to uphold the Constitution and to preserve the integrity and sovereignty of the Union and that forms of oath in the Third Schedule to the Constitution should be suitably amended for the purpose. It is proposed to give effect to these recommendations by amending Clauses (2), (3) and (4) of Article

19 for enabling the State to make any law imposing reasonable 44 restrictions on the exercise of the rights conferred by sub-clauses (a), (b) and (c) of Clause (1) of that article in the interests of the sovereignty and integrity of India...'

In other words, before the 16th Amendment came into force, it was ostensibly legal to preach and propagate even secession from India. In the wake of the defeat in the Sino-India war in 1962 there was an atmosphere of nationalistic fervor that enabled the state to proscribe regional aspirations that were articulating, if not secession from India, but far more autonomy for the states.

Thus, in the first 13 years of the founding of the Indian Republic, the freedom of speech and expression was abridged twice. In its final avatar now, Article 19(2) reads: 'Nothing in sub-clause(a) of Clause(1) shall affect the operation of any existing law, or prevent the State from making any law, in so far as such law imposes reasonable restrictions on the exercise of the right conferred by the said sub-clause in the interests of the sovereignty and integrity of India, the security of the State, friendly relations with foreign states, public order, decency or morality or in relation to contempt of court, defamation or incitement to an offence.'

There is a need to revisit these restrictions and even Article 19 itself. The word 'citizens' needs to be replaced with people given the number of Indians who are a part of the global diaspora and have a view on what goes on in India. A substantive number of them are not Indian citizens, including people who have heft in the public discourse. The amended Article 19 must read as follows: 'All people will have the right to freedom of speech and expression throughout the territories of India. This right would include the freedom of the press. It includes within its ambit the right to offend. Those offended by the exercise of this right, including and not limited to the state, would have the right to exercise all the remedies available under the various laws for the time being in force.' Clause 2 of Article 19 must be repealed.

This would dispel the spectre of some of the draconianism while preserving the rights of the state and the people. It would then pave the way for reinterpreting defamation, contempt and privileges insofar as they proscribe, circumscribe and punish free speech.

The Asian Age
18 February 2017

FREEDOM TO OFFEND IS INTRINSIC TO FREE SPEECH

The mugging of free speech in Ramjas College is reprehensible. However, what is even more abhorrent is the manner in which Union ministers are in an overdrive, trying to justify both the violence and viciousness. It is ironic that the finance minister, while speaking at the London School of Economics and Political Science, an institution with a global reputation for both critical inquiry and unrelenting critique, sought to rubbish the Indian academia by claiming that there is an 'alliance of subversion' across university campuses in India.

His colleague, the minister of information and broadcasting, has been tilting at windmills in a manner that would make even Don Quixote turn in his grave. However, most repugnant has been the conduct of my friend, the junior minister of home affairs, who has chosen to intimidate a young student who has the conviction of courage to stand up to ideological vehemence unleashed by the diabolic forces of right reaction and national subversion.

What the FM perhaps forgot or, maybe, was oblivious of, is that he was speaking in a country that had upheld its right to free speech at even the gravest times of national peril. Its Parliament functioned throughout World War II; its media was not gagged while a bipartisan war cabinet strove to surmount the Nazi-Fascist-Imperial Axis.

Perhaps the finance minister was selectively amnesiac of the fact that not very far away from where he was speaking, on 9 February 1933, the Oxford Union, the undergraduate-debating society of Oxford University, passed a notorious motion: 'This

House would not in any circumstances fight for King and Country.' It was carried by 275 votes to 153.

Though Winston Churchill termed the vote as 'abject, squalid, shameless' and 'nauseating', and it was even speculated that it misled the German Dictator Adolf Hitler into hallucinating that Britain had lost the resolve to fight. Nobody, much less the British government, charged the students with sedition.

The vote certainly did not reflect either the will or the mood of the British people. The Oxford undergraduates were young people, who often liked to take stances or a controversial position precisely because they recognized that it would provoke a robust reaction - as the Oxford vote indubitably did.

When war finally came in 1939, many of those who had taken part in the debate and voted for the motion did indeed fight - and die - for king and country. Does the Indian finance minister believe that the then British government erred and all those recalcitrants who voted for the motion should have been locked up under the law on sedition, which Britain in any case was freely using in India to chill the freedom of speech and expression? Yes, the British can be accused of double standards, but isn't that the case with all occupying powers?

However, what the Finance Minister's remarks and the information and broadcasting minister's verbosity do reflect is a 'deep-seated' paranoia that an instinctive 'alliance of subversion' is indeed crystallizing across university campuses, and this alliance of progressive, pluralistic and nationalistic forces is predicated on undermining the governance paradigm of the current BJP-led NDA government.

The specious debate on nationalism that the government and its fellow travellers keep periodically provoking is nothing but a pathetic attempt to deflect attention from their administrative and governance failures. One can only laugh at these attempts because it raises a very basic question

- was the whole of India anti-national before PM Narendra Modi and his not-so-merry men assumed office? Why did such a debased debate not defile the hallowed portals of our democratic edifice earlier? The answer is very simple: Because no sanguine people and no self-assured nation need to wear their patriotism on their sleeves. For as Samuel Johnson articulated as far back as 7 April 1775: 'Patriotism is the last refuge of a scoundrel.'

Even on Kashmir, the manner in which an alternative viewpoint articulated by none other than the former home and finance minister is sought to be savaged is a telling reflection on how the current dispensation believes in lynching the messenger. The situation in the valley is like a tinderbox. The next flash may send it over the precipice, perhaps irretrievably.

The seriousness of the situation has been underscored by none other than an independent panel of citizens led by the venerable Yashwant Sinha - the finance and foreign minister in the Vajpayee government.

As a distinguished editor very aptly put it, if any individual can qualify to fit the definition of the term 'deep state', then certainly Chidambaram fits the bill in its entirety.

If two separate avatars of the deep state, P Chidambaram and Yashwant Sinha, are saying the same thing, the government would dismiss their concerns at its own peril.

However, at the very heart of the lumpenism and vandalism perpetrated by the ABVP in Ramjas College lies a fundamental question: Does the right to freedom of speech and expression include the right to offend? And it certainly does, and while the offended, including the state, can invoke remedies available under the law if reasonable restrictions prescribed in Article 19(2) of the Constitution are transgressed, does the alleged offender have protection from state-sponsored intimidation, violence and coercion - especially the *bhakts*, perverts and trolls – while the law takes its own course? That is the question civil society must ponder over.

The Economic Times
4 March 2017

SHOULD CONSTITUTION BE AMENDED TO MAKE FREEDOM OF SPEECH A DIRECT FUNDAMENTAL RIGHT?

The Constitution of India does not formally recognize the freedom of the press. Article 19 of the Constitution proclaims the 'protection of certain rights regarding freedom of speech':

'All citizens shall have the right to freedom of speech and expression; to assemble peaceably and without arms; to form associations or unions; to move freely throughout the territory of India; to reside and settle in any part of the territory of India; and to practice any profession, or to carry on any occupation, trade or business.

The Constitution caveats the freedom of speech and expression with the following all encompassing restrictions that are prone to expansive, ambiguous and self-serving interpretations.'

'Nothing in sub clause(a) of clause(1) shall affect the operation of any existing law, or prevent the State from making any law, in so far as such law imposes reasonable restrictions on the exercise of the right conferred by the said sub clause in the interests of the sovereignty and integrity of India, the security of the State, friendly relations with foreign States, public order, decency or morality or in relation to contempt of court, defamation or incitement to an offence.'

There is a further joker in the pack and that lies in the form of

Article 19(6) that circumscribes the right among other things to carry on any trade or business. The question, therefore, that remains open to malicious construal is whether newspapers, broadcasting, radio and even social media are an exercise in freedom of speech and expression or are business or trade subject to restrictions under Article 19(6).

This is precisely the insidious distinction that the CBI sought to draw when they put out a press release stating they had raided the office and business premises of the promoters of NDTV and not its newsroom.

In other words, attempting to suggest that they were not interfering with the freedom of the press but merely trying to probe/investigate/regulate the back-end or the business end of the commercial enterprise called NDTV. The relevant excerpt from the statement reads: 'It is clarified that searches have been carried out at the premises of the promoters and their offices based on search warrants issued by the Competent Court. CBI has not conducted any search of (the) registered office of NDTV, media studio, newsroom or premises connected with media operations. CBI fully respects the freedom of press and is committed to the free functioning of news operations.'

As a lawyer and a former minister of Information and Broadcasting, I can only say with a reasonable degree of authority that not only is this the most vile hairsplitting, it is also extremely side-splitting. When you have to squeeze a media company you do not attack its news operations; instead, you go for the jugular by cutting off its revenue streams and put its business activity under a microscope, all the while sending it private messages that if your news coverage falls in line then the government will make the bad stuff go away. This is the executive's standard operating procedure when it lets its hounds loose on a media organization.

But the Supreme Court has held in a catena of decisions

that the business end of a media enterprise is intrinsically and organically linked to freedom of speech and expression. As far back as 1961 regarding the *Sakal* newspaper, a Constitution bench of the court laid down the law that holds the field even today.

It reads: 'The only question that would then remain would be whether the impugned enactment directly impinges on the guarantee of freedom of speech and expression. It would directly impinge on this freedom either by placing restraint upon it or by placing restraint upon something, which is an essential part of that freedom. The freedom of a newspaper to publish any number of pages or to circulate it to any number of persons is each an integral part of the freedom of speech and expression. A restraint placed upon either of them would be a direct infringement of the right of freedom of speech and expression.'

It therefore is evidently clear that any unwarranted attack on the commercial aspect of a media enterprise that is based upon 'obtained complaints' and actuated by malice, paranoia or executive schizophrenia is a direct, unmitigated and sledgehammer assault on freedom of speech and expression.

Now contrast the Indian constitutional scheme with the American constitutional position. The First Amendment to the US Constitution protects the Freedom of the Press in its entirety. It reads: 'Congress shall make no law respecting an establishment of religion, or prohibiting the free exercise thereof; or abridging the freedom of speech, or of the press; or the right of the people peaceably to assemble, and to petition the Government for a redress of grievances.'

Thus the estoppel is absolute. The US Congress can enact no law that abridges the freedom of the press in any manner much less let loose the hordes of Chengiz Khan – the law enforcement and investigative authorities – to bludgeon a media house into subjugation. The US Congress passed this amendment along with eight others making up the Bill of Rights as far back as 15 December 1791.

These 45 words encompass the most basic of American rights: freedom of religion, freedom of speech, freedom of the press, the right of assembly, and the right of petition.

The First Amendment was not important in American life until well into the 20th century. The meaning was not clear even in 1791 but the intent was. Notwithstanding such unambiguous intent the words still are the subject of continuing interpretation and dispute even in the 21st century.

Therefore, to obviate any sinister sophistry about Article 19(1)(a) in the Indian Constitution, which the CBI craftily came up with, perhaps the time has come for India to amend its Constitution and include the freedom of press as a direct right in the chapter on Fundamental Rights, rather than a derivative freedom of the right to speech and expression. This would obviate any attempts by the right-wing, the left-wing or centrist authoritarian figures to endanger this basic, natural and inviolable right.

The Indian Express
13 June 2017

TERROR LIVE ON TV PUTS EVERYBODY IN DANGER

The Dhaka terror attack that claimed scores of innocent lives has, once again, focused attention on the role of the media, specially the electronic media, in situations like these. Bangladesh Prime Minister Sheikh Hasina was withering in her criticism. She said: 'When we are taking preparations, channels were telecasting these live. Do they not think the terrorists were watching and devising their strategies accordingly? I request television channel owners to not do this.' She went on to add: 'In the United States, when people were killed, neither CNN nor BBC showed anything to jeopardize the operations. But in our country, there is competition between television channels. Some channels don't want to listen.' In the same vein, she delivered a not-too-veiled threat: 'I can issue the licence, and I can revoke it as well. This is not a childish game.' Sheikh Hasina urged TV owners to show the bad side of militancy: 'It's the responsibility of all.'

This isn't the first time a person holding a responsible office has articulated the exasperation of the state with the electronic media's role in such circumstances.

In November 2008, while the terror attack in Mumbai was still going on, a similar scenario had played itself out. TV channels competed relentlessly with each other to cover every second of the attack. Preparations and plans of the security forces were broadcast live, giving the attackers' Pakistan-based handlers vital information that allowed them to give updates and instructions to their merchants of death on the ground. One channel even broadcast a live phone interview with one of the terrorists at Chabad House, while he was engaged in the grisly task of butchering innocent people held hostage there.

In the aftermath of 26/11, there was consternation with many strategic and counter-terrorism experts taking the media to task for endangering the lives of not only the security personnel involved but also the innocent people holed up inside hotels and other places under assault by the terrorists.

Guidelines in the form of an advisory on how to cover an evolving terrorist outage were repeatedly issued to the TV channels by the information and broadcasting ministry, but they are observed more as an exception than a rule.

Even the Supreme Court severely criticized the media coverage of 26/11. In the judgment confirming the death sentence of Ajmal Kasab, it observed: 'From the transcripts, especially those from Taj Hotel and Nariman House, it is evident the terrorists who were entrenched at those places and more than them, their collaborators across the border, were watching the full show on TV.'

The court further added that it was not possible to find out if the security forces actually suffered any casualty or injuries due to the way their operations were displayed on TV screens. But it was beyond doubt that the way their operations were freely shown made the task of the forces not only very difficult, but also dangerous and risky.

Any attempt to justify the TV channels' conduct by citing the right to freedom of speech and expression would be totally wrong and unacceptable in such a situation. The visuals shown live on TV channels could also have been shown after the terrorists had been neutralized. But in that case the telecast wouldn't have had the same shrill as well as chilling effect, and wouldn't have shot up the channels' TRP ratings. It must, therefore, be held that by covering live the attack on Mumbai in the way it was done, the TV channels weren't serving any national interest or social cause, but simply acting in their own commercial interests, and putting national security in jeopardy. The coverage of the Mumbai terror attacks by the mainstream electronic media has done much harm to the argument that any regulatory mechanism for the media must only come from within, the Supreme Court held.

While this may be the view of the state as represented by the executive and judiciary, the fourth estate has another view, one that also needs to be taken on board. Media organizations argue that a terrorist attack is 'news' and, therefore, it is their responsibility to cover it holistically in real time. The fact that viewership shoots up at such times is not due to their endeavour to monetize an unfortunate situation, but primarily because of the desire of people to remain updated about the situation.

Media industry bodies and self-regulatory mechanisms contend it is extremely unfair to put restrictions on such coverage given that freedom of speech and expression is a treasured national maxim, even though with some caveats. It should, therefore, be left to the media organizations to determine their individual red lines than be subject to the coercive regulations of the state. The other argument that is put forth is that while it may be easier to regulate and monitor the mainstream media, how would governments stop the dissemination of citizen-generated live feeds both visual and text on the Internet and social-media platforms, given the technological advances and the miniaturization of the instruments of information dissemination.

When told that their counterparts in the West display far more sensitivity and restraint while covering such events, whether 9/11 or the recent Paris, Brussels or even Istanbul attacks, they just shrug it off saying the media habits in each country are different. Can this really be put down to a cultural thing, or is it the commercial thing at work?

There is enough empirical evidence to suggest that media mores in South Asia are distinctive as revenue models in most countries that have a shrill dog-eat-dog ethos are non-existent. However, can that justify the competition for eyeballs during monumental national catastrophes? It also brings to the fore another key issue: Should this restraint, whether by the state or self-enforced, be limited only to terrorist situations and other national security imperatives, or should it also extend to natural disasters?

There is an urgent need to find a golden mean on this issue. It would be advisable that the media itself take the lead before it is too late.

The Asian Age
9 July 2016

DON'T MISUSE HOUSE PRIVILEGES TO MUZZLE PRESS

'The framers of the Constitution knew that free speech is the friend of change and revolution. But they also knew that it is always the deadliest enemy of tyranny. Freedom of speech means that you shall not do something to people either for the views they have, or the views they express, or the words they speak or write. Only a free and unrestrained press can effectively expose deception in government. And paramount among the responsibilities of a free press is the duty to prevent any part of the government from deceiving the people. The press was to serve the governed, not the governors...' These words of United States Supreme Court Justice Hugo Black are more relevant today in India's context than perhaps the day they were penned for preserving and upholding the freedom of the press guaranteed under the First Amendment to the United States Constitution.

The press may be the fourth pillar of democracy. But a press that is not free is no press. A press that cannot criticise those is power is no press. A press that is intimidated by political power or sucks up to it is no press. For even our constitutional scheme recognises the freedom of speech and expression, and therefore by implication the freedom of press. However, more often than not, political parties in India irrespective of their ideology seek to proscribe the free press, for their collective DNA is thin-skinned to censure. Even though to do so is constitutionally amoral.

The recent decision of the Karnataka Assembly in sentencing journalists Ravi Belagere and Anil Raju to imprisonment for one year for contempt of the House and a member, and therefore breach of privilege of the House, is unfortunate, to say the least.

It is not that legislative bodies in the past have not acted in this manner earlier too and their decisions have been held to be constitutional abridgements. Déjà vu. In 1964, the UP Assembly found one Keshav Singh of being guilty of contempt of the House and the members of the House, and sentenced him to a week in prison. Keshav Singh's crime was similar to the one that Mr Belagere and Mr Raju are charged with – writing stuff that was considered by the UP Assembly to be defamatory to one of its members.

When Keshav Singh applied for and obtained bail from the Allahabad High Court, the Assembly went one step further and sought to imprison the advocate who filed the bail petition and the two judges who granted bail. The entire Allahabad High Court consisting of 28 judges unanimously, and in a mark of solidarity, stayed the operation of the sentence passed by the UP Assembly. The unprecedented situation was surmounted only when the President made a reference to the Supreme Court. In the presidential reference, the Supreme Court observed: 'In conclusion, we ought to add that throughout our discussion we have consistently attempted to make it clear that the main point which we are discussing is the right of the House to claim that a general warrant issued by it in respect of its contempt alleged to have been committed by a citizen who is not a member of the House outside the four walls of the House, is conclusive, for it is on that claim that the House has chosen to take the view that the judges, the advocate and the party have committed contempt by reference to the conduct in the habeas corpus petition pending before the Lucknow bench of the Allahabad high court. Since we have held that in the present case no contempt was committed either by the judges, or the advocate, or the party respectively.'

The court therefore was clear that criticism, even if unwarranted, does not constitute either contempt of the House or its members, thus allowing them to invoke the yet uncodified privileges under Articles 105 (3) for Parliament and Article 194 (3) for the state legislatures. The privileges need to be spelt out in black and white. Over the years, the Supreme Court has repeatedly laid down the law circumscribing the powers and privileges of the legislatures.

The freedom of the press is the heart of social and political intercourse while privileges of the legislative institutions are one of the undefined silences in the text of the Constitution, and have been exculpated and transported into the Indian Constitution straight from the traditions of the House of Commons.

The object of parliamentary privileges is to ensure that the smooth functioning of legislative institutions is not hampered. The power to sentence to imprisonment for the contempt of the House or its members is undoubtedly a privilege of the House, a power that has been exercised by the House of Commons in the past, but when the Supreme Court of India has categorically held that actions outside the House, which have no direct effect of impinging on the functioning of the legislative chamber, cannot be a trigger for invoking constitutional privileges, is it then justified for the House to punish journalists whose opinions may be unpalatable or in the worst case even slanted or downright defamatory? The answer is no.

The Karnataka Assembly has overshot its constitutional mandate under Article 194 in sentencing Mr Belagere and Mr Raju for publishing some articles. An article being disrespectful to a member or the House cannot be cause for the invoking the power of privilege, specially when it is in exercise of the basic human right of free speech. This is more so when such an action for such alleged defamation would find remedy in both civil and criminal law, in the nature of a defamation suit or a criminal complaint, coupled with a prayer for injuncting such person from publishing such defamatory material in future. It is in this context the exercise of the constitutional power of parliamentary/ legislative privilege, and to find guilty a journalist of contempt of the House would tantamount to giving a special status to a member of such a legislative body and providing him or her a remedy apart from what is prescribed by law. The privilege to punish for the contempt of the House is a power that must be scarcely called into use in the most extreme of situations when the majesty or the functioning of the House is under stress or severe strain. Allegedly defamatory writing hardly falls into that category.

The judicious use of a constitutional privilege becomes all the more relevant when a wave of tyranny has been unleashed by the BJP government against independent sections of the media.

Orchestrated repression by the state – if you are not with us, then you are against us – has divided the Indian media into the 'kept' and the 'unkept' media.

On the one hand, broadcasting entities that are functioning in a manner that make even North Korean TV channels blush with shame are patronised by the government, and those who speak truth to power are being hounded and persecuted.

In such a situation, any action by any constitutional body that reinforces this spectre of fear, repression and intimidation is avoidable, even though that may not have been the intent at all in this particular case and the journalist duo just managed to get under the skin of some members of the House.

The Karnataka Assembly would therefore be well-advised to suo motu withdraw its resolution.

The Asian Age
8 July 2017

State of the Nation

ELECTION RESULTS DO NOT SET THE STAGE FOR 2019

As I write this piece from Berlin - detached from the hype and hoopla that marks the declaration of any election result - the main question that comes to my mind is this: Does this result set the stage for the general elections in 2019? The answer is no.

Here's why I say this: The BJP has won UP and Uttarakhand convincingly. The Congress has retained Punjab and has emerged as the single-largest party in Manipur and Goa. The AAP has to cope with a sense of disappointment for they were hopeful in Goa and sanguine in Punjab.

Now, let us now rewind to 2002. That year, no party got a clear majority in UP. The Congress won Punjab and Uttarakhand and was the single-largest party in Goa and Manipur.

Did that election set the stage for the 2004 general election? No. The riots in Gujarat in 2002 did. This fact was admitted by none other than former Prime Minister Atal Behari Vajpayee after he lost the 2004 parliamentary elections.

Similarly, in 2007, the BSP won in Uttar Pradesh. The Akali Dal-BJP alliance routed the Congress in Punjab. The BJP won Uttrakhand. The Congress, which won Manipur, was the single largest party in Goa.

Did this election set the stage for the 2009 parliamentary polls? No. The Indo-US civil nuclear deal did. It helped the

Congress catapult from 145 seats to 206.

Again in 2012, the SP won UP. The Akali Dal-BJP alliance retained Punjab and won Goa. The Congress won in Manipur and emerged as the single-largest party in Uttarakhand.

Did this election provide the platform for the 2014 Lok Sabha polls? No. What provided the focus was Narendra Modi's anointment as the prime ministerial candidate in Goa in 2013. It helped the BJP resolve its internal contradictions that had befuddled it for nine long years and to unite under the leadership of Narendra Modi.

Is the 2017 result also an amalgamation of diverse state-level impulses?

While data would have to be crunched to analyse why the poll numbers have once again defied exit-poll calculations, this result does provide headroom for Modi to try and address the two fundamental challenges that plague India: The first is India's relationship with Pakistan, and the second, the faltering economy, notwithstanding the creative statistics that have been put out by the Central Statistical Organization.

Would Modi be willing to pick up the threads in India's relationship with Pakistan that has been on the rocks since the Uri attack, or will he wait since Pakistan is scheduled to go for national assembly elections in 2017?

If he chooses the latter, it means that the zero-sum game between the two countries will continue till the May of 2019.

Coming to the economy, the fact remains that we have entered an era of jobless growth. Given the youth bulge in our demographics, this is a potentially dangerous portent that can have long-term implications for social stability and cohesion.

Modi's real test will be in Gujarat later this year. In the meantime, this amalgam of state-level factors at work gives him a chance to refocus on governance.

As far as the Opposition is concerned, they should focus on finding a presidential candidate who commands credibility across the widest spectrum of forces hostile to the current dispensation.

Only then would it be back in the game.

Hindustan Times
11 March 2017

INDIA NOW YEARNS FOR A STRONG OPPOSITION

It has been three weeks since the results of the last round of Assembly elections were announced. If there is one emotion that grabs you in every conversation, it is fear. There is a sense of foreboding that we are heading towards becoming a one-party state. You can smell the apprehension; you can feel the anxiety; and you can breathe the trepidation.

Let me give you three vignettes from three different conversations. At an event in Gurgaon, I came across a young woman who was beside herself with anger. Wagging an accusing finger almost into my face, she hissed: 'How could you allow this government to walk all over you...? This country requires a strong Opposition,' followed by a long diatribe of how bad we were, but why we were also most needed at the moment.

The second was at a dinner the next day hosted by an influential promoter of an infrastructure company in Mumbai. As soon as I walked in, a high-profile media mogul from the entertainment industry exclaimed: 'Where are you guys? You cannot allow this country to degenerate into a one-party state! It would be a disaster for India. This country requires a strong Opposition. Get your act together.'

The third was on a train from Chandigarh. A retired general who was sitting next to me said: 'I have advised my children not to come back to India as this country is turning into a totalitarian state.' He then added: 'Why are you chaps rolling over and playing dead? This country needs a balance in its polity, and that can only happen if the Opposition is robust.'

What do these three stray conversations tell you? In less

than three years, a country that was yearning for a strong government is now desperate for a strong Opposition.

It is not the minorities alone who are feeling petrified. They are possibly resigned to their fate as second-class citizens in today's India. Many prominent members of the minority communities, who have served India with distinction, have articulated their anguish publicly.

Oxymoronically, it is the great Indian middle class that is now feeling insecure with the electoral choices they have made. Remember that the middle class in any society is a very vocal opinion-maker. The UPA lost the middle class in 2010, and even all the work that it had done for the poor, the downtrodden, and the marginalized could not resuscitate it politically in 2014, including and not limited to lifting 190 million people out of poverty irrespective of the benchmark that you use.

This triumphant vigilantism is not the only problem. 'Hubris' is a word Greek origin that has many meanings, but in the current context, it translates into arrogance of power. It emanates out of delusions of grandeur and manifests itself in the relationship that the ruler wants to have with the other institutional stakeholders in the power dynamic.

For the past 34 months, the standoff between the executive and the judiciary has been the most telling example of this hubris - a relationship that has become more tenuous after the Supreme Court struck down the National Judicial Appointments Commission Bill.

Another example is the relationship the prime minister wants to have with the fourth estate. There he finds a soulmate in US President Donald Trump, who has refused to attend the White House correspondents' dinner as he was cut up with the pushback from the media over some of his more idiosyncratic utterances, and his minions have also chosen to boycott it in solidarity.

In November 2013, at the International Film Festival of India in Goa, I had prophesied that a great evil would soon stalk our land and that evil would come in the form of illiberalism and a constriction of India's creative spaces. I had cautioned the assembled practitioners of the 'arts' that an extremely bruising battle for the very soul of India would soon unfold. There is only a limited amount that writers, thinkers, and artistes can do.

The real heavy lifting has to be done by the political class. The starting point is to rededicate themselves to the foundational values of the Indian republic. For over the next 26-odd months, the fight for the founding vision of India will be fought again. In 1947, there were two philosophical postulates that confronted India - either to be a Hindu Pakistan or a modern and a pluralistic nation. The latter construct triumphed, much to the disappointment of the right fundamentalists, for whom a religious partition was synonymous with the total exchange of populations.

In their moment of triumph, they now want to unravel the manner in which the Indian nation-state has been constructed over the past seven decades. The names doing the rounds for the post of President of India, despite the denials, are symptomatic of that effort.

However, this has made large sections of India very uneasy, used as they are to a very amorphous form of governance of their private spaces. Herein lies the opportunity for the Opposition.

Rather than being ashamed or diffident, it needs to squarely fight the battle for India's constitutional underpinnings, articulated in the Preamble. For that, they need to shed diffidence and, most important, the fear of saying the right thing, even though there may be perceived electoral implications for doing so. They need to smell the coffee: No longer is this nation yearning for a strong government; it is crying out for an effective Opposition.

The Asian Age
1 April 2017

ABOLITION OF TRIPLE TALAQ IS AN IDEA WHOSE TIME HAS COME

The lawyers have argued, the judges have heard the lis, the media has reported it blow by blow and now everybody waits with bated breath for the day of reckoning. Will these three words and the underlying practice be held to be illegal by a Constitution bench of the Supreme Court or not?

If I was a betting man I would wager most certainly they would, notwithstanding the arguments put forth by the proponents of this practice that courts should not interfere into matters of faith that stretch far back into millennia. For if this argument was valid then the progress of humankind would have languished somewhere in the Stone Age. The fact remains that the only constant in the march of the human civilization is change.

Religious conservatives throughout the long evolution of the human race have been fiercely resistant to change. Nothing exemplifies it better than the resistance by the Catholic Church to even the translation of the Bible into languages easily understood by the people.

Roman Catholicism decreed Latin as a holy language. Ordinary people were given strictly limited access to the Bible, and it had to stay that way. This stand provided the clergy control over the masses. They did not want regular folks pottering in spaces they circumscribed as their own territory. The Catholic order unquestionably recognized that several of its instructions were based, not on the Bible, but on church tradition. Undoubtedly, this was one of the reasons for their averseness to permit their faithful to have access to the Bible. By merely reading it, people would become mindful of the contradictions between church canons and scripture.

Thus, as far back as 1079, in response to the request made by Vratislaus, Duke of Bohemia, seeking permission to use the Slavonic language in local church services, Pope Gregory VII pronounced, 'We cannot in any way grant this entreaty.'

Later in 1559, Pope Paul IV circulated the first catalogue of books proscribed by the Roman Catholic Church. It banned possession of the Bible renditions in Dutch, English, French, German, Italian, and Spanish, as well as some in Latin. Anyone who desired to study the Bible was told to obtain permission in writing from bishops or inquisitors – not an alluring possibility for those who wanted to remain above suspicion of heresy.

People who ventured to own or disseminate the Bible in the everyday language of their expanse had to cope with the wrath of the Catholic Church. Many were incarcerated, burnt at the stake, roasted on spits, condemned to life in prison, or dispatched to the galleys. Appropriated copies of the Bible were scorched. Indeed, Catholic priests persisted on impounding and burning copies of the Bible well into the 20th century.

Similarly, in the medieval and obscurantist Indian ethos, the highest aspiration for a woman was a convoluted commitment to the virtues of pureness, and fidelity to the husband. From this belief stemmed the ritual in which a wife was almost divinely ordained to immolate herself on the funeral pyre of her deceased husband as evidence of this devotion.

The underlying rationale for this abhorrent practice was that by sacrificing herself a widow saves herself from the wretched existence of widowhood and therefore bizarrely ends the hazard she posed to society. Those days a widow was not allowed to remarry, nor was she permitted to turn to religious scholarship, and thus condemned to a miserable and harsh existence. It was drilled into the psyche of women, since infancy, that the pain of the pyre was less agonizing than the torment she would endure physically and emotionally for the rest of her life as a widow.

Raja Ram Mohan Roy was the first Indian to protest against this horrendous custom. In spite of protests from orthodox Hindus, he carried on his crusade against this ghoulish ritual. Finally, he was able to convince Lord William Bentick, the Governor General of India, who promulgated a law in 1829 abolishing the custom of Sati by making it illegal and punishable as culpable homicide. If it would not have been for the conviction of courage of this brave soul, Hindu women may still have been burning on the pyres of their husbands in cremation grounds across our great land.

A century and some decades later in the flush of a liberation tainted by partition in 1947, as the makers of modern India settled down to draft the Constitution of India they were confronted by the abhorrent practice of untouchability that was institutionalized in the Hindu faith. A person belonging to the lowest rung of the religious pecking order was considered to be so inauspicious that even if his mere shadow fell on people higher up in the social order amounted to sacrilege.

With one stroke of the pen the founding fathers inserted Article 17 into the Constitution of India and abolished this demeaning outrage. Article 17 states: 'Untouchability is abolished and its practice in any form is forbidden. The enforcement of any disability arising out of Untouchability shall be an offence punishable in accordance with law.'

The Civil Rights Act of 1955 implemented this constitutional fiat. Now this reform did not come from the wellsprings of the Hindu faith. Religious bigots did argue that this faith-based practice actually preceded the Indian Constitution practically by a couple of thousands of years and therefore could not be done away with even by the supreme law of the land. However such retrogressive diatribes did not deter the framers of the

Constitution from doing what was right. Had they not acted possibly untouchability would have been prevalent even today.

At the other end of the spectrum lay the erstwhile rulers of the princely states who believed in their special, inherited privileges till perpetuity. But Article 363(a), inserted into the Constitution on 28 December 1971, stripped them of their titles, privy purses and immunities. The rationale was simple. All citizens, irrespective of his or her station in life, are equal in the eyes of the law. Several of these erstwhile Maharajas and minor princelings, including those epitomes of debauchery, argue that these privileges were hard won honours in battles waged in the past and must enjoy constitutional protection.

But the rising tide of egalitarianism knows no boundaries. Although, it's a pity that some of the dishonourable descendants of these disempowered people still cling onto the pitiful vestiges of that decadence.

To conclude, the relentless march of the movement for gender justice ordains that the abolition of triple talaq is an idea whose time has come. Either the self appointed custodians of the faith can do it voluntarily or the courts or legislation will most certainly do it for them.

The Indian Express
22 May 2017

TIME HAS COME FOR A GRAND BARGAIN ON AYODHYA DISPUTE

On 30 May 2017, senior BJP leaders Lal Krishna Advani, Murli Manohar Joshi and Uma Bharti appeared before a trial court in Lucknow to stand trial in the Babri Masjid demolition case. For these accused eminences, the frenzied events of 6 December 1992 must represent a paradigm far removed in space and time from their current pre-occupations and reality.

Perhaps these criminal proceedings were not the retirement many of them were looking forward to in their sunset years. Especially LK Advani – who took the BJP from a two-seat party in 1984, to 88 seats in 1989 and then onwards to the BJP's first enduring coalition government at the Centre from 1999 to 2004 – must be intrigued at the turn of events, if not understandably bitter.

Advaniji may wonder for the remainder of his very golden years, and may God give him a very long life, as to whether bailing out Narendra Modi on that fateful plane ride with Atal Behari Vajpayee in April 2002 to Panjim, Goa, to attend the party's National Executive Meeting, was perhaps the biggest political blunder of his long and distinguished career.

For him, the timing of the current summons couldn't have been more ominous, coming as they have just ahead of the Presidential elections. The stance taken by the CBI counsel in the Supreme Court, which ordered an expeditious day to day trial, could not have been possible, without both explicit knowledge and instructions of the Prime Minister, to whom the CBI directly reports.

For, if anyone out of the BJP deserved to be the President of

India, it is Mr Advani. It is another matter that a lot of folks, including this writer, are opposed to anyone from the RSS/BJP gracing that august office.

A host of other BJP leaders must be equally petrified today, as they have read the tea leaves very well. The one-and-a-half man oligarchy which rules the country can also turn on any of them at any point of time.

Enough of the present, however. It is time to turn the blood-stained pages of this most sordid saga in contemporary Indian history. It all began again on 1 February 1986, when District and Sessions Judge of Faizabad KM Pandey ordered the padlocks of the disputed Ram Janmabhoomi-Babri Masjid structure, which had been sealed for 37 years since 1949, to be reopened. He also ordered that access be granted to the idol of Ram Lalla mysteriously installed there since that fateful Thursday night of 22 December 1949.

Though a number of stories claim that the opening of the padlock was a command performance at the behest of the erstwhile Central government, led by Congress Prime Minister Rajiv Gandhi, the Liberhan Commission which subsequently enquired into the demolition of the Babri Masjid and its attendant circumstances for 17 long years - incidentally, at the cost of Rs 9.02 crore — found that to be untrue.

The unlocking triggered another round of anger, agitation and grief. The BJP/RSS and its many allied organisations sensed an opportunity for political revival and decided to up the ante. They launched a nationwide agitation for the removal of the mosque and it's replacement by a temple. Consecrated bricks, Ram *shilas,* were mobilized from thousands of villages, to be used in its construction.

The Ram Janmabhoomi movement polarized India, culminating in the destruction of the mosque on that fateful day of 6 December 1992. The demolition unleashed a round of bloody communal riots across the country, laying the ground for the serial blasts that rocked Mumbai in March 1993 and spawned the first indigenous Islamist terror organisations.

For the next decade or so, from 1992-2002, the Ram temple matter went on the backburner. But when a trainload of karsevaks aboard the Sabarmati Express had an altercation with Muslim vendors at Godhra railway station in February 2002, it seemed as if its ghostly apparition was raising its head again. In a horrendous turn of events, the burning of coach S-6 claimed 59 innocent Hindu lives.

The rest, of course, is history. The erstwhile Gujarat government allowed the dead bodies to be brought to Ahmedabad. In his testimony to the Nanavati Commission in August 2004, then DGP PC Pande said: 'When I got to know that about 58 bodies were being brought to Ahmedabad or that they have already [been] brought, at that time I had a feeling, that looking to the communal situation of Ahmedabad...(which) is sensitive and like a tinderbox...in the prevailing circumstances if these dead bodies are brought to Ahmedabad then possibly it will create serious impact...'

A ghastly pogrom followed. It scarred and mutilated the soul of India, compelling then prime minister Atal Behari Vajpayee to remind present Prime Minister Narendra Modi about his *raj dharma*. No description can capture the poignancy of Vajpayee's stern warning to Modi that is available on YouTube. It is a must watch.

The Gujarat pogram led to the birth of the Indian Mujahedeen, which was aided and abetted by the Lashkar-e-Taiba, the ISI, and HUJI. At this time it consisted of students, most of them Kashmiris, studying in Deobandi madrasas in south Gujarat, Andhra Pradesh, Karnataka and Maharashtra. Recruitment videos of Islamist terror organisations began to make plentiful references to the riots. They radicalized a lot of otherwise irreligious Muslim young men.

Now all this may seem like old hat but this chronology bears testimony to the destructive potential of energizing communal fault lines and laundering historical grievances, especially in the age of digital communication and social media.

The continuing legal saga around the Babri Masjid demolition will serve no other purpose but resurrect old ghouls and buried phantoms from the blood-tainted past, thus sparking off even more violence. It only serves those who have built their political careers on polarization to keep India on edge and keep emphasizing the otherness of those who disagree.

The time has come for a grand bargain on the Ram janmabhoomi-Babri Masjid dispute. We must let go of the past. If we keep uncorking the poisoned chalice of history it will only consume us. As for the ensuing court proceedings, in the larger national interest they may perhaps serve no tangible purpose.

The Indian Express
2 June 2017

IS IT REALLY ABOUT BEEF, THOUGH?

The recent overdrive of the Haryana police, presumably on the instructions of the state government, to check for beef allegedly mixed in biryani consumed or sold in the state's Mewat region on the eve of Eid-al-Adha has yet again triggered an unfortunate controversy and entails an equally tragic tale of events.

If what happened on the intervening night of 24 and 25 August 2016 in the village of Dingerheri is true - that two men were murdered, another two critically injured and two women gang-raped by members of the Gau Raksha Samiti (cow protection committee) - along with the startling information that the police are working overtime to sweep the facts under the carpet, it only underscores the warped sense of priorities of the BJP government and its instrumentalities.

Why the Silence Now, Modiji?

One of the two victims poignantly related at a press conference in Lutyens' Delhi: 'They (attackers) asked us, "You eat cow meat? We said no." They said, "You eat cow meat." They said, "We are killing you because you eat cow." We told this to the police but they are not doing anything.'

Why is the silence of the Prime Minister so deafening barely a month after he grandiloquently declared at a town-hall interaction: 'It makes me angry that people are doing business in the name of cow protection. Most of them are anti-social elements hiding behind the mask of cow protection... I will ask the state governments to prepare a dossier on such people as 80 per cent will be found involved in anti-social activities, which no society would approve of.'

Simply translated, it means that the Prime Minister believes 80 per cent of these *gau rakshaks* (cow vigilantes) are goondas.

Now, Modiji, some of these goondas you have referred to have allegedly butchered two people, critically injured two more, and criminally assaulted two young women barely 50 kilometres from your residence in New Delhi, but there is not even a tweet from you? Assertive action is a long shot; action condemning this barbaric and heinous assault that strikes at the very root of the idea of India. Freedom of culinary choice is part of the right to life guaranteed by Article 21 of the Constitution that you have sworn to protect and defend four times as chief minister and once as the Prime Minister.

The Story Doesn't Add Up

The Haryana Gauvansh Samrakshan and Gausamvardhan Act 2015 is yet to be tested on the touchstone of its constitutionality. Even if it is held intra-vires by any court of law, how would it square up with the judicial pronouncements of various Indian courts? For instance, most recently, the Bombay High Court on 7 May this year held that a ban on imported beef (in this case from outside Maharashtra) would be an 'infringement of the right to privacy, which is a fundamental right'.

The Bombay High Court further laid down that under Article 21 of the Constitution, citizens are protected from unnecessary state intrusion into their homes. The court also struck down a provision in the Maharashtra Animal Preservation (Amendment) Act 1976, which put the burden of proof on the person found to be in possession of beef. The court declared that this too infringes on the fundamental rights of a person.

Which is why the actions of the Haryana Police are even more bizarre; their story simply doesn't add up. Rather than investigating a complaint of alleged cow slaughter and then trying to establish a nexus between its consumption or sale, the state, in the absence of a valid complaint or possibly on the basis of trumped up complaints, is going sniffing around in biryani handis with the clear intent of intimidating and terrorizing an already subjugated and fearful minority.

Thus, it can only be concluded that this is not about beef, it is about majoritarianism. Ever since the BJP government took office at the centre, there has been a continuous and calibrated attempt to demonize the minorities, particularly the Muslims. From Ghar-Wapsi to Love Jihad, statements declaring that minorities are second-rate citizens to defining nationalism in pulp-patriotic terms and the ubiquitous beef bans are attempts to impose a warped right-wing template on the nation.

It is an attempt to anchor the public discourse 90 degrees to the right. It is an attempt to demolish the pluralistic idea of India and replace it with a theocratic ethos. It is an attempt to validate the two-nation theory of Jinnah. It is an attempt to PakistanizeIndia.

RSS-BJP's Age-Old 'Divide and Rule' Trick

Then, there is the cynical political imperative that the RSS-BJP believes in - that polarization fetches electoral dividends. The lynching of Mohammad Akhlaq in Dadri during the Bihar elections on the ostensible insinuation that he possessed beef and the subsequent front-page advertisements by the BJP extolling the cow was perhaps the crudest manifestation of desperation for gains at the hustings. The fact that the electorate of Bihar repudiated these attempts at ghoulish politics does not seem to have taught the 'powers that be' in New Delhi a lesson.

The recent incidents of Quran-tearing in Malerkotla in Punjab - a place protected by the divine benediction of the tenth Sikh

Guru Gobind Singhji, which remained largely peaceful even during the darkest hours of Partition, when all of Punjab burned in the fire of communal frenzy - and now the state-sponsored beef vigilantism in Haryana, are both aimed at splitting society in neighbouring Uttar Pradesh that has an unfortunate communal past.

For there are hardly any Muslims in Punjab to bring about any significant polarization that can pay electoral dividends. It is a 'Mohammad Akhlaq Part II' now being played out in Haryana with Uttar Pradesh as the target, just as Dadri was sought to be made the flash point for Bihar by abusing the power of the hyper-media age that we live in.

What the prime minister and the chief minister of Haryana do not understand is that coming as it does after the alleged mass rapes in Haryana during the Jat agitation that are being enquired into by the Punjab and Haryana High Court and the deluge that drowned out Gurgaon, it is sending a signal to the world that mayhem and anarchy are omnipresent in the immediate vicinity of the national capital.

Narendra Modi must remember money is the biggest coward - it finds the safest haven. It does not go to places where chaos and anarchy prevail. You can either have your beef vigilantism or your foreign investment. You cannot have both.

The Quint
11 September 2016

INDIA IS SIMMERING, NOT SHIMMERING

'*Modiji ke mukable mein koi nahin hai* (Modi has no challenger).' Thus spake Nitish Kumar, Chief Minister of Bihar, the neo-convert to the NDA camp when asked about the possible outcome of the 2019 Lok Sabha elections. But come 2019 or even earlier, the Chief Minister may have to eat his words if not his hat.

Notwithstanding the deployment of North Korean television channels to script a narrative of invincibility around the BJP, the systematic insinuation, innuendos and downright lies about the Opposition leaders as well as the routine abuse and misuse of investigative agencies and the law enforcement machinery, the fact remains all is not well on the ground.

India is not shimmering, it is simmering. The Bharat-India cleavage has widened to an unprecedented degree. The disconnect between the ground narrative and the public discourse is nothing short of hallucinatory.

There is unprecedented farm distress in the country. As many as 12,602 persons involved in the farming sector - 8,007 farmers and 4,595 agricultural labourers - committed suicide in 2015, according to figures provided by the Union government to the Supreme Court. Union agriculture minister Radha Mohan Singh told Parliament that according to the National Crime Records Bureau data for 2016, which is yet to be published, 11,400 farmers committed suicide; in 2015, the number was 12,602.

From Tamil Nadu to Mandsaur in Madhya Pradesh and even in the food bowl of Punjab, falling farm incomes are driving farmers to take the extreme step of ending their lives.

Similarly, the industrial scenario is dismal. In June 2017, eight core sectors of the economy grew by a dismal 0.4% , down from 7% for the corresponding month in 2016. The growth in Index of Industrial Production (IIP) was 1.7 per cent in May 2017, as compared to a growth of 8.0 per cent in May 2016.

As opposed to 380 lakh new jobs that India required in the 38 months this government has been in office, job creation or job growth for 2015 and 2016 (April-December) stood at 1.55 lakh and 2.31 lakh in numbers respectively. The former minister for rural development Jairam Ramesh recently underscored this worrying downturn when he said, 'In the first two years of the Modi government, only 4.4 lakh jobs were created in the organized sector as opposed to 21 lakh jobs created during the first two years of the UPA II government.'

Demonetization and the implementation of the flawed GST have further broken the back of the informal sector of the economy leading to widespread chaos. The GDP growth numbers evidence this phenomenon. In the fourth quarter of 2016 the economy clocked only 6.1% which, with 2004-05 as base year translates into a measly figure of 4.1% only.

Social harmony has been torn to shreds with Hindustan acquiring the notorious sobriquet of Lynchistan - all thanks to the active encouragement and support of the ruling dispensation, notwithstanding the pro-forma condemnation by the Prime Minister once in a while. It does not require rocket science to discern the truth. You only need to ask why these lynchings weren't taking place from 2004-14 and why have they become a norm these past three years?

Internal security lies in tatters. Kashmir is up the creek without a paddle. It is a volcano waiting to erupt again as it did last year after Burhan Wani was killed by the security forces last year. Maoist militancy is on the rise. From 1 January to 15 July, 170 deaths in 504 incidents took place. The Northeast is on the boil with the Gorkhaland violence having peaked this summer. The 47-day-long shutdown, which started on 15 June, is the longest so far in the picturesque hill station which had last witnessed a 40-day bandh in 1988 by the Gorkha National Liberation Front and a 44-day shutdown in 2013 by Gorkha Janmukti Morcha on the statehood issue. Even in the otherwise peaceful state of Tripura, the Indigenous People's Front of Tripura has upped the ante on their demand to carve out Tipraland – a separate state from Tripura. Meanwhile, there is no sign of the fabled Naga Accord.

However, the gravest threat today is to India's external security. Perhaps, for the first time in the past seven decades the nation is staring at a two-front situation with an aggressive Pakistan and a belligerent China breathing down our neck with only ten days of war fighting reserves at our disposal. It would be a strategic blunder to take Chinese president Xi Jinping's threats lightly. A conflict, limited or otherwise, seems imminent at a time and place of China's choosing. How prepared is India materially, morally, physiologically and logistically beyond the rhetoric of muscular nationalism? Even on the benchmark of hyper-nationalism, the current government says one thing in New Delhi and does another tango with Pakistan on the sidelines of a security conference in Moscow.

Is all this reality lost on the people of India? Is Modi the pied piper of Hamelin leading the nation over a cliff with people more than willing to do his bidding? The answer is a Big No. People are waiting, like they did in 2004, to speak through the ballot boxes – when Shining India was unleashed upon them by the late Pramod Mahajan and Vajpayee bit the dust. What is even worse today is the trampling of fundamental freedoms and the spectre of an undeclared emergency that looms large over the country. A great evil stalks our land. People understand that it has to be vanquished under any circumstances.

All that it requires is a lightning rod to crystallize that anger and it will emerge in the next 12 months. Remember Modi also emerged as a challenger in 2013 less than a year before the 2014 elections; today, we still have an effective twenty months to go. Nitish Kumar could have been that lightning rod, but he blinked, probably miscalculating that a bird in hand is better than two in the bush.

However fortune always favours the brave as many of us learn at our own peril. Nitish Kumar's moral courage quotient is on the anvil.

The Indian Express
2 August 2017

NOTA: A BAD IDEA FOR INDIRECT ELECTIONS

On 24 January 2014 and subsequently again on 27 January, the Election Commission issued an administrative direction that the "None of the Above" (Nota) provision would be made applicable for elections to the Council of States (Rajya Sabha) also. It clarified the process of voting by another directive on 12 November, 2015.

Somehow this administrative direction escaped the attention of lawmakers until it got flagged during the run-up to the election in Gujarat scheduled for 8 August 2017.

Though the Supreme Court has refused to stay the use of Nota in the Gujarat Rajya Sabha elections, it has nonetheless agreed to examine the constitutional validity of the Election Commission's administrative diktat.

To put things in perspective, the Supreme Court in PUCL vs. Union of India 2013 directed the use of Nota in the context of direct elections to the Lok Sabha and the respective state Assemblies. The judgment delineated that in a direct election a voter must be given an option to choose 'None of the above' to express their dissatisfaction with all the candidates/ political parties on the ballot.

In this judgement the court observed: 'Universal adult suffrage conferred on the citizens of India by the Constitution has made it possible for these millions of individual voters to go to the polls and thus participate in the governance of our country.' Accordingly, the court directed the EC to provide necessary provision in the ballot papers/EVMs for providing the Nota button. Subsequently, necessary amendments were made in the respective statutes to give effect to the orders of the court.

On the other hand, when it comes to electing members to the Rajya Sabha, Article 80(4) of the Constitution provides for indirect election by the members of the legislative Assembly of a state in accordance with the system of proportional representation by 'a' single transferable vote.

Further, Section 59 of the Representation of the People Act 1951 provides for the manner of election:

At every election where a poll is taken, votes shall be given by ballot in such manner as may be prescribed, (and, save as expressly provided by this Act, no votes shall be received by proxy) (Provided that the votes at every election to fill a seat or seats in the Council of States shall be given by open ballot.)

The use of Nota in indirect elections is thus, in direct conflict with and militates against the system of proportional representation by means of the single transferable vote envisaged by the Constitution, the Act and the Rules.

The use of Nota cannot be sanctioned by way of a circular dated January 24, 2014, which in any event cannot override the provisions of Article 80(4), the provisions of the Act and the Rules. In any event, the use of Nota cannot be made applicable without the necessary amendments in the Act and Rules. It is fairly evident therefore, that the system of Nota makes the system of proportional representation by means of the single transferable vote meaningless, cannot be made applicable in Rajya Sabha elections.

In matters of election to the Rajya Sabha, MLAs are also duty bound to support the candidate put up by the political party to which they are affiliated.

In Kuldip Nayar vs Union of India (2006) 7 SCC 1; a

Constitution bench of the Supreme Court categorically observed that the declarations under Form 2-B read with 2-C binds the MLAs to vote for the candidate set up by the political party to which they are affiliated. The court further emphasised the rationale behind proportional representation and the need for maintaining the sanctity of members of the political party by ensuring party discipline.

The ruling held: 'It cannot be forgotten that the existence of political parties is an essential feature of our parliamentary democracy and that it can be a matter of concern for Parliament if it finds that electors were resorting to cross-voting under the garb of conscience voting, flouting party discipline in the name of secrecy of voting. This would weaken party discipline over errant legislators. Political parties are the sine qua non of parliamentary democracy in our country and the protection of party discipline can be introduced as an essential feature of the purity of elections in case of indirect elections. Parliamentary democracy and a multi-party system are an inherent part of the basic structure of the Indian Constitution...'

While upholding the validity of an open ballot, the court categorically observed: 'owing to the impugned amendment... a voter has to disclose the way he has cast the vote to the representative of his party.'

The court also deprecated the practice of cross-voting in the Rajya Sabha elections and held that it is the duty of Parliament to take cognisance of the misbehaviour and misconduct and legislate remedial measures for the same. Breach of discipline of political parties for collateral and corrupt considerations removes the faith of the people in a multi-party democracy.

In view of the categorical observations of the court in the Kuldip Nayar case rendered in the context of the Rajya Sabha elections, no direction ought to have been given by the commission to introduce Nota, which has the effect of not only upsetting and destroying the nature of proportional representation by means of single transferable vote but also will have the effect of breaching party discipline by virtually amending the 10th Schedule of the Constitution of India (anti-defection law) through an administrative order thereby diminishing the importance of political parties which the court has held to be a part of the basic feature of the Constitution.

The Asian Age
5 August 2017

Kashmir Conundrum

J&K WAITING FOR AN EMOTIONAL OUTREACH

As the all-party delegation prepares to head for Srinagar, it will be confronted with the spectre of the Valley still smouldering like a powder keg, perhaps waiting for the next match. Though curfew restrictions have been eased, a clueless BJP-NDA government at the Centre and a paralysed PDP-BJP government in Jammu and Kashmir continue to run around like headless chickens trying to catch their own tail.

The question India needs to ask is: why should the death of a self-professed militant trigger an outpouring of unrest that refuses to go away? Why should children under 15 be pelting stones at the symbols of the state, ready to face the wrath of pellet guns in return? What is this new ogre the Indian nation is confronted with?

The current Frankenstein is unfortunately one of our own creation. A child born in 1989-90 in the Valley will be 26 years old today. During the transition from childhood to adolescence, and then finally adulthood, s/he will have seen conflict and chaos as the natural order of things.

Now extrapolate it to someone who was 10 or 15 years old in 1990, and you have two generations of young Kashmiris for whom curfew, cordon and search, street protests, azadi, AK-47, AK-56, Pakistan-trained mujahids and enforced disappearances, torture, interrogation, and encounters, fake or real, are as much a part of the everyday lexicon as school, college, ice cream, career, and dating are for youngsters in any normal part of the world.

Myth, rumour, folklore, history and institutional memory bring these words to life and direct anger and bitterness towards the men in khaki or olive green. Perhaps this is the only enduring face of the Indian state they have seen. It is, therefore, unsurprising that over 14 per cent of those with debilitating pellet injuries are under 14. The closest parallel is Afghanistan, where violence has been the new normal since 1980.

In the 26 years since the current violence began in the Valley, the media paradigm has seen a transformation. Private cable and satellite TV have come of age and, more important, Internet and new media platforms have become both sources of information exchange and a vent for the young and others to channelize their angst and annoyance.

However, the noxious steam that is released re-circulates in the overheated pressure cooker called Jammu and Kashmir, ratcheting up pressure to explosive levels. It blows the lid at regular intervals, and the poisonous brew overflows like a deluge. That is what happened in 2008, in 2010 and again in 2016. Each time, the trigger may have been different but the result was the same, leaving India rummaging to put together a response and invariably tilting at windmills.

Today, Prime Minister Narendra Modi and Home Minister Rajnath Singh keep parroting the clichéd *'insaniyat, jamhooriyat and Kashmiriyat'* line, without trying to understand what these words really mean. Rather than applying balm, therefore, these phrases end up having the same effect and impact as the ubiquitous 'triple talaq'.

On 18 April 2003, when then Prime Minister Atal Behari Vajpayee used these words from the rostrum of the Sher-e-Kashmir Stadium, he extended the hand of friendship to both

Pakistan and the people outside the mainstream in J&K. By then, he had understood after many false dawns that there could be no meaningful dialogue with the separatists without concurrent confabulations with Pakistan. Most of them had a symbiotic relationship with the Pakistani establishment in varying degrees. While some were on a tight leash, others enjoyed a slightly longer rope, but the cord was always omnipresent.

The assassination of Hurriyat leader Abdul Ghani Lone a year earlier in May 2002, when he spoke out against the foreign militants and in favour of a dialogue, asserting that the militant gun had no justification in Kashmir, may have solidified Mr Vajpayee's belief that the separatists and the 'deep state' in Pakistan were conjoined as Siamese twins.

Similarly, when the UPA government took office, Prime Minister Manmohan Singh followed the twin tracks of exploring with Pakistan's President Pervez Musharraf the modus vivendi of making borders irrelevant in J&K, while holding out an olive branch to splittists in the Valley.

Contrast this with the situation now, where Mr Modi has decided to deploy the rhetorical arsenal of Pakistan-occuoied Kashmir, Gilgit-Baltistan and Balochistan to surmount a disastrous Pakistan policy. This has only further queered the pitch of bilateral relations. No wonder that despite Rajnath Singh's tweeting the clichéd mantra of this government, he didn't get a chance to play host to a single separatist leader of any consequence during his recent stay at the Nehru Guest House in Srinagar.

Pakistan's decision to send 22 MPs to different countries to raise the Kashmir issue with their interlocutors, ahead of Pakistan PM Nawaz Sharif's annual pilgrimage to 'the Mecca of talk shops' - the UN General Assembly session in New York later this month - is only going to make the gobbledygook between the two countries even more vile.

This will feed right back into the Valley's pressure-cooker ecosystem, further estranging the populace. It is slowly becoming a redundant oxymoron that Kashmir requires a political solution. What is the political solution a 14-year-old is looking for when he pelts stones? What the state needs is an emotional outreach to people under constant stress - a regular conversation with the rest of India that creates an emotional bonding. A jackboot on the door and the cold tip of a gun in the ribs certainly don't create the ambience for such a conversation.

In every counterinsurgency doctrine, winning the hearts and minds of the populace is a core objective. It involves the simultaneous application of both hard and soft power by the state. However, in Kashmir's case, the soft touch has either been conspicuous by its absence or too faint to make any tangible impact.

What India hasn't grasped despite handling countless insurgencies is that till the time a separatist impulse has popular partisan support and the oxygen of the media, it is impossible to surmount. J&K has both these ingredients in abundance: an angry young population with the power of new media to boot. It's a deadly cocktail, to say the least.

The Asian Age

3 September 2016

AFTER FOUR INCIDENTS, BACK TO SQUARE ONE

Four unfortunate incidents over the past one month and India and Pakistan are back to normal – at each other's throats. It all depressingly began again with the chief of the Pakistani Army, Gen. Qamar Javed Bajwa, confirming the death sentence of Kulbhushan Jadhav handed down by an opaque general court-martial process. Almost concurrently, the confirmation coincided with the disappearance of a retired lieutenant-colonel of the Pakistan Army, Habib Zahir, in Nepal. His last reported whereabouts were in the Buddhist pilgrimage town of Lumbini. Then there was a terror attack on an Indian Army camp in Kupwara that led to the death of three Indian Army jawans, including a captain.

This was followed by the barbaric beheading of two Indian soldiers, Naib Subedar Paramjit Singh, a 42-year-old junior commissioned officer with the 22nd Sikh Regiment, and 45-year-old head constable Prem Sagar of the BSF's 200 Battalion, who were ambushed by a Border Action Team of the Pakistan Army and decapitated on the Line of Control in the Krishna Ghati Sector in the Poonch district of Jammu and Kashmir.

This incident took place right after the Pakistan Army Chief ostensibly visited Haji Pir on April 30.

With the television media in India in an overdrive and competitive jingoism being unleashed by the Pakistani media too, the only winners of this zero sum game are the prophets of doom who thrive on hostility, hatred, conflict and chaos.

For the Pakistani civilian government that otherwise pays lip service to the cause of peace between the two countries, this standoff is a welcome distraction after the pyrrhic Supreme Court victory in the Panama Papers case. However, for the Indian establishment, these portentous developments come at a time when there is a dangerous drift in the internal security situation.

The situation in J&K has gone belly-up for the lack of a better word. Stone-pelting has become the everyday norm rather than the exception. Banks are being looted on a daily basis. The voter turnout in the recent Srinagar bypoll was an abysmal seven per cent, down from a high of 65.5 per cent in the Assembly elections held in the autumn of 2014.

The Election Commission had to cancel the Anantnag parliamentary bypoll because the security situation is extremely volatile and non-conducive to a free and fair democratic franchise.

All these developments underscore one basic fact – that the experiment of ideological incompatibles BJP and PDP has proven to be a non-starter. Nothing underscored this failure better than the extremely poignant lament of Chief Minister Mehbooba Mufti after her meeting with Prime Minister Narendra Modi: 'We are where Vajpayee left us,' she bemoaned.

The Chief Minister obviously did not have the courage to say that the situation during the 10 years of the United Progressive Alliance was far better, for to do so in the current atmosphere would be nothing short of blasphemy.

However, it may just be worth recalling the roller coaster ride that the India-Pakistan relations went through during the Vajpayee era, specially after the Agra Summit held in July 2001.

For those who may have forgotten, that after the attack on the Indian Parliament on 13 December 2001, Prime Minister Atal Behari Vajpayee publicly vowed there would be an *aar paar ki ladai* (a fight to the finish). His Cabinet Committee on Security greenlighted the largest-ever mobilisation of the Indian Army after the 1971 war. The deployment, code-named Operation Parakram, saw a million men and women on both sides of the border staring each other down eyeball to eyeball.

In the midst of this unprecedented tension another terrorist attack, this time on an Army camp in J&K, almost tipped the balance. On 14 May 2002, near the town of Kaluchak, three militants attacked a tourist bus from Himachal Pradesh and killed seven people. After that they entered the family quarters of the troops and fired indiscriminately at the inmates, killing 23 people, including 10 children, eight women and five soldiers. The age of all the children killed ranged from four to 10 years. Thirty-four people were injured in the attack. Incidentally, the next attack of this magnitude on a military camp happened 14 years later on 19 September 2016, in Uri, that left 17 soldiers dead and almost two-dozen injured.

The Kaluchak outrage sent alarm bells ringing across the world. In New Delhi the embassies of Western powers ordered the evacuation of all non-essential personal. The 'N' word was bandied about carelessly on both sides. Back-channel persuasion by the US and other influential powers had a salutary effect on both countries. The US and their allies were heavily committed to Afghanistan. They did not want a full-scale escalation between two nuclear weapon states to add to their bundle of woes. After 10 months of mobilization, the Indian Army was asked to stand down and return to its barracks without a shot being fired. The Indian Army lost over 1,800 officers and men during this operation. In reply to a question in the Rajya Sabha on 30 April 2003, then defence minister George Fernandes stated: 'The number of Army personnel killed or wounded in J&K and the western sector during the mobilisation, Operation Parakram, from December 19, 2001 to October 16, 2002 was 1,874.'

Finally, on 18 and 19 April 2003, Mr Vajpayee travelled to

Srinagar where he extended an olive branch to both the Hurriyat and Pakistan simultaneously for he had figured out in the five years of his prime ministership till then that the separatist movement in Kashmir could not be untwined and dealt with separately. It had been tried, but a number of Hurriyat leaders who had mustered the courage of striking out on their own had been assassinated by the deep state in Pakistan.

That initiative led to the ceasefire agreement of 25 November 2003, which by and large held the field throughout the UPA years, only to be rudely shattered in September 2014, when unprecedented firing from both sides started off and is still continuing along the international border, Line of Control and the Actual Ground Position line (AGPL).

Fifteen years later, the summer of 2017 bears an eerie resemblance to the summer of 2002. India-Pakistan relations are at a nadir, jingoism is at its peak, negotiating space is getting constricted. The 'N' word is irresponsibly invoked on television channels by hawkish former military officers from both sides. The difference, however, is that the situation in J&K in 2002 was better than it is today. A new PDP-Congress government under late Mufti Mohammad Sayeed had assumed office and there was hope of a better future in the air, which is not the case today.

Though Mr Modi and his strategic team feel that they are on top of the situation, they would be well advised to revisit those fateful years and draw a leaf out of former Prime Minister Vajpayee's book, who was fond of saying that you cannot choose your neighbours. He told Parliament on 23 April 2003: 'I assured the people of Jammu and Kashmir that we wish to resolve all issues – both domestic and external – through talks. I stressed that the gun can solve no problem; brotherhood can. Issues can be resolved if we move forward guided by the three principles of *insaniyat* (humanism), *jamhooriat* (democracy) and *Kashmiriyat* (Kashmir's age-old legacy of amity). In my speech, I spoke of extending our hand of friendship to Pakistan. At the same time, I also said that this hand of friendship should be extended by both sides. Both countries should resolve that we need to live together in peace.'

Perhaps, like Mr Vajpayee, it would take Mr Modi also another few years to learn this lesson – by then it may be too late. The wheel of democracy can behave rather quirkily that Prime Minister Vajpayee too discovered to his peril.

The Asian Age
13 May 2017

IRAN'S KHAMENEI NAMES KASHMIR, CALLS FOR JIHAD

Even before the holy month of Ramzan could conclude and Eid spread its munificent blessings over the valley of Kashmir, a deputy superintendent of the Jammu and Kashmir police was stripped, brutally assaulted and killed on the premises of the Jamia Masjid in Srinagar. Just as the faithful had gathered to mark the Shab-e-Qadr or the Night of Power, Mohammed Ayub Pandith's body was dragged out of the mosque and dumped in a drain.

Only six weeks ago, on 10 May, Lt Ummer Fayaz was abducted by militants and killed in Shopian district. Even as the pall-bearers carried the body of the slain soldier to a nearby orchard, the mourners talked in whispers about the marks of torture on Ummer's back, his broken jaw, crushed ankles, his missing teeth, and the bruises and cuts on his body.

The lynching and the gruesome murder of both officers made the nation recoil in horror. Justified outrage and calls for retribution filled the airwaves.

Growing up on the front lines of another battle against terror, this time in Punjab in the 1980s, and having lost a parent to the depredations of that ghastly violence, the ongoing violence in Jammu and Kashmir is but a sickeningly familiar story of brutalization, and dehumanization of society's psyche brought about by the endless cycle of violence.

Perhaps, we should try and imagine the mindset of a child who was born in 1990 in Kashmir and is today 27 years old. All that he has seen in his life are curfews, cordon and search operations, stone pelting, enforced disappearances, and torture and fake/real encounter killings. For him, violence is the new normal. The face of the Indian state is someone clad in olive green or khaki carrying an AK-47, kicking the front door down. This is the dominant narrative in any militancy-prone, terror-infested, defiant area - give it any label of your choice.

In such an environment of fear, terror, intimidation, coercion and death lurking around the corner, it is easy for the likes of Burhan Wani to become folk heroes and legends. As the *Washington Post* said about him 'Burhan Wani was just 22 when he died, but he was already a folk hero to many in Indian-administered Kashmir. The telegenic insurgent – a leader of a group designated a foreign terrorist organisation by the State Department – played his social media persona to the hilt, mugging for pictures with automatic weapons and posting videos on WhatsApp and Facebook exhorting other men to join the separatist cause. He also threatened attacks on police convoys and military housing.'

There were others after him. Sabzar Ahmad renowned as 'SAB DON', became the new poster boy of terror in the Kashmir Valley. Taking forward the cult of Wani, Ahmad guided Hizbul terrorists until the security forces neutralised him in an encounter on 27 May. More such poster children will, unfortunately, emerge, the reason for which is not difficult to discern.

Some months ago about 40-odd young people from various districts of Kashmir, under the aegis of an organisation called Jammu Kashmir People's Alliance that has an interesting tagline, 'We serve, We settle,' came to meet a Concerned Citizens Group in Delhi. This is led by former finance and external affairs minister Yashwant Sinha, who led two highly visible and successful outreach initiatives to estranged sections in the Kashmir valley.

During the talk these young boys and girls told us a very

disturbing story. Apparently among the most wanted stone-pelters in the valley is a gentleman called 'DK' and he is all of SEVEN years old. If the average age of stone-pelters is between 7-17 years, irrespective of who is paying them, the Indian state is sitting on a volcano that is belching lava but has not really exploded. When and if it does, a lot of people entrusted with the remit of handling Kashmir both at the Centre and in the state, will not have the time to say goodbye.

Then there is an international dimension to the Kashmir situation that has suddenly manifested itself. It has everything to do with the turmoil that US President Donald Trump's visit to Saudi Arabia has plunged the Islamic and Arab world into. The calling out of Qatar for its links with Iran and subsequent developments have further divided the already fractured polity of the Middle East.

On Eid, the Supreme Leader of the Islamic Republic of Iran delivered a very chilling address in Teheran. Ayatollah Ali Khamenei publicly called for Jihad. 'According to Islamic jurisprudence, when an enemy takes over Muslim lands, jihad in any possible form becomes everyone's duty,' he said. 'Palestine is the number one issue of the Islamic world, but some Islamic countries are acting in such a way as if the Palestinian case had been ignored and forgotten,' he added.

Then came the coup de grace. 'Muslims the world over should also openly support the people of Bahrain, Kashmir and Yemen and repudiate oppressors and tyrants who attacked people in Ramadan,' Khamenei said.

Though Iran has earlier voted against India on the issue of Kashmir in the Organization of Islamic Cooperation (OIC), this is the first time the situation in the Valley has been given a religious colour by Iran's Supreme leader. Even those who are fighting against the Indian establishment in some districts of J&K have refrained from labelling their movement as 'Islamic', much less 'jihadi'.

It is only one or two Hizbul Mujahideen 'activists', Zakir Rashid Bhatt among them, who have tried to give militancy an Islamic colour. In a video that went viral, he said, 'When we pick up stones or guns it should not be with this intention that we are fighting for Kashmir (as a nation). The sole motive should be for the supremacy of Islam so that Shariah is established here.'

But Zakir Bhat was quickly denounced by the other separatist leaders.

However, the fact that a Shia religious leader of Iran has clubbed Kashmir, a predominantly Sunni area with causes like Yemen and Bahrain should worry New Delhi, because Iran backs up its rhetoric with logistical support, be it to the Hezbollah, Hamas, Islamic Jihad or the Houth is in Yemen, to name but a few.

This support from Iran coincidentally comes at a time when the predominantly Sunni ISIS, or Daesh, is trying to strike roots in Jammu and Kashmir.

On his forthcoming visit to Israel, Prime Minister Modi would be well advised to ask his interlocutors about the activities of General Qasem Soleimani, the once reclusive head of the Revolutionary Guards and its elite Quds Force. General Soleimani has suddenly surfaced from an era in the dark leading clandestine processes overseas, to attain virtually an iconic stature in Iran. He and the Quds Force have successfully converted erstwhile territorial struggles into religious battles. One can only hope that Kashmir is not their next frontline.

The government should abandon its excessive reliance on hard power in J&K. Hard power should only be used to soften the recalcitrant so that soft power can take over. Jammu and Kashmir is crying out for the healing touch. All the leaders of the state cutting across the political divide, including chief minister Mehbooba Mufti, are urging the Central government to initiate an outreach to the alienated.

The Prime Minister will ignore their sage advice at his own peril. Terms like 'final solution' do not help, as that may mean very differently from what the Central government has in mind.

The Indian Express
29 June 2017

Economic Downturn

JUNK FAILED MODELS, FOCUS ON THE 99 PER CENT

The annual ritualistic presentation of the Budget is an overhyped event to say the least. It provides the Finance Minister with an opportunity to grandstand and wax eloquent on each and every issue. Voluminous documents are churned out commencing with the Economic Survey to something called an outcome Budget. This government did well by breaking with tradition and junking the antiquated practice of presenting a standalone Railway Budget.

The government would do well if it limits the Union Budget to a barebones income and expenditure statement and allows every minister to present his plan of work to Parliament based upon a prior allocation of resources. The standing committees must then examine the budgetary allocations of every ministry in conjunction with the annual plan of work. It would make the whole exercise far more meaningful than the process currently in play.

However, what the Union Budget does even in its current avatar is that it provides an opportunity to re-examine the fundamental macroeconomic model. However, the Economic Survey of 2017 waxes eloquent when it propounds: 'The result of all these reforms over the past 25 years has been a remarkable transformation of India from a largely closed and listless economy to the open and thriving economy that we see today. The country's progress is not only qualitative, it is also measurable.' Consider, for example, four standard measures: openness to trade, openness to foreign capital, the extent to which public-sector enterprises dominate commercial activities and the share of government expenditure in overall spending.

However, this is far from the truth. In a recent report, Oxfam has stated that eight men own the same wealth as 3.6 billion people who make up the poorest half of humanity.

In a follow-up interview, Nisha Agrawal, CEO, Oxfam India, said: 'In 2016, India is the second-most unequal economy after Russia. Inequality is fracturing our economy and the reality is that today 57 billionaires control 70 per cent of India's wealth. Even the International Monetary Fund recently warned that India faces the social risk of growing inequality...'

Oxfam's Ms Agrawal further stated:

'Over the last 25 years, the top 1 per cent has gained more income than the bottom 50 per cent put together. Far from trickling down, income and wealth are being sucked upwards at an alarming rate. Like many other countries, in India, too, policies have not focused on raising the incomes of the poorest. India's liberalization in the early 1990s has seen an explosion in inequality since it created opportunities in a few high-end sectors such as banking, IT, telecom and airlines that only created a handful of jobs for the highly skilled and educated. Not many policy reforms have happened either in agriculture or labour-intensive manufacturing that could have created millions of jobs and raised incomes of the poor. Furthermore, not much effort has been made to raise more revenues and spend on basic education and health so that the poor could benefit from the opportunities being created.'

It does not require rocket science to know the truth of those assertions. Anyone who has travelled extensively around the country over the past two-and-a-half decades has seen the disparities grow at an exponential pace, notwithstanding attempts to bring about socio-economic equity by successive governments.

Just as the command economy model locked India into the derided 'Hindu rate of growth', the current economic construct has failed to deliver sustainable livelihood to a substantive swathe of people in India. Explaining what that model is, the Economic Survey of 2017 points out: 'India has replaced its erstwhile socialistic vision with something resembling the "Washington Consensus" open trade, open capital and reliance on the private sector - essentially the same development model that has been tried and proven successful in most countries of Eastern Asia. Reforms along these lines have been adopted by every successive Indian government over the past quarter of a century.'

While it may have worked for the Asian tigers because of smaller populations or other locational and geographical factors, the dividends of this economic model for India have been few and far between. It is the oligarchs and crony capitalists who have thrived and flourished, much like the initial flush of Russian economic liberalization. The question then is - where do we go from here?

The answer lies in part in one of the chapters of the Survey, 'Universal Basic Income: A conversation with and within the Mahatma.' Explaining what the concept means, the Survey says:

'Universal basic income is a radical and compelling paradigm shift in thinking about both social justice and a productive economy. It could be to the 21st century what civil and political rights were to the 20th. It is premised on the idea that a just society needs to guarantee to each individual a minimum income which they can count on, and which provides the necessary material foundation for a life with access to basic goods and a life of dignity. A universal basic income is, like many rights, unconditional and universal: it requires that every person should have a right to a basic income to cover their needs, just by virtue of being citizens.'

With the state unable to provide jobs or even opportunities for stable and sustained employment, the time has come to build an economy for 99 per cent of the people, and not just a few at the very pinnacle of the pyramid.

It would entail a fundamental restructuring of the economy that does not look at this construct as a dole to keep the unwashed masses from revolting against a skewed economic order but as a means of harnessing the creative energies of millions of our people by putting them to work. With the palliatives of socialism and the 'trickle-down effect', both having failed, universal basic income benchmarked by the index of gross national satisfaction must be the way forward.

The Asian Age
4 February 2017

WHY IS AIR INDIA BEING SINGLED OUT FOR STEP-MOTHERLY TREATMENT?

In colloquial Hindi there is a ribald saying - *'Garib Ki Joru Sab Ki Bhabhi'* - which while it defies literal translation, points to the helmsmen of a sputtering economy who have suddenly woken up and now want to burnish their neo-liberal credentials. The easiest mark to pick on is none other than the national airline, Air India. An abused child whose parents keep turning on it periodically.

The in-principle Cabinet approval for the privatisation of Air India begs a fundamental question that policymakers as well as the gurus of privatisation have failed to address in the past 26 years: Does privatisation serve the public interest?

To answer this question one must go back into the genesis of the current phase of the 'grand garage sale' of public assets callously bartered away to oligarchs for nothing more than a song accompanied by the mocking melody, 'It is not the business of government to do business.'

It all began with the Conservative Party in Britain in the 1970s. The Tories had long been obliged to undertake some process of de-nationalization. In response to the protracted political crunch in which the Tories struggled to maintain their parliamentary numbers, the Ridley report, written by one of their MPs, Nicholas Ridley, recommended a policy of breaking up the public sector and dismembering unions.

Privatisation was at first subordinate to other policy themes, the most prominent being wage suppression to control inflation.

In Ridley's assessment, trade union muscle in the UK was meddling with market forces and triggering inflation, which therefore had to be checked to restore the cost-effectiveness of Britain. He and other Conservative MPs also saw it essential to neutralize the power of unions in the wake of the collapse of the Edward Heath government, as a consequence of the strike by coal miners in 1974.

In 1979, soon after she became prime minister, Margaret Thatcher proposed de-nationalization as a potential panacea for the recession that followed. The guiding canon was that privatisation would make the large utilities more productive – a euphemism for profit – thereby making English capitalism competitive in comparison to its continental counterparts.

The first Thatcher government privatised several large public sector companies, namely British Aerospace, Cable & Wireless, Jaguar, British Telecom, Britoil and British Gas, thereby commencing a wave of privatising core utilities around the world.

This bizarre belief in privatisation soon became a global pandemic. Throughout the world, governments ceded to the oligarch's control of everything – electrical utilities, prisons, railroads and even education systems. Soon, sales of state owned enterprises worldwide had totaled over $185 billion – with no signs of stopping.

In the year 1990 alone, governments sold $25 billion in state-owned enterprises. The largest single deal occurred in Britain, where investors paid over $10 billion for 12 provincial electricity firms. New Zealand sold more than seven state-owned companies, including the government's telecommunications company and printing office, for a value that topped $3 billion.

Emerging economies were quick to jump on the privatisation bandwagon, usually to align them with the neo-liberal economic order but at times also to raise revenue. Argentina carried out a major privatisation exercise that included among other things the sale of its Telephony, national aviation and petrochemical companies for more than $2.1 billion. Mexico did the same to reduce the size and operating cost of the public sector that brought a windfall of $2.4 billion.

Over the next decade, privatisation was at the top of the economic agenda of Russia and the newly democratized countries in Eastern Europe. Public assets were virtually gifted away to all shades of robber barons. In 1990 alone, the Treuhandanstalt – a public trust mandated by the German government with the task of privatisation, arranged the sale of more than 300 companies for approximately $1.3 billion.

However all this wanton play with taxpayers money led to intense introspection when the worldwide revolt against globalization reached a crescendo in the wake of the great economic meltdown of 2008. By then it had become evident that widespread privatisation and private ownership of public enterprises did not necessarily translate into improved efficiency or even better quality of public service.

Most importantly the arbitrage, derivatives and leverages driven economic catastrophe established that private sector managers have no compunctions moral, ethical or even legal about pursuing mindless profit-making strategies and corporate practices that eventually brought down the global financial system itself.

Dominant in the privatisation debate has been the appropriate role of government in a social democracy. The laissez-faire school views governments as an unwarranted and inflated encumbrance on an otherwise effectual systems; while critics believe that government is a critical component in a system in which profit cannot be the only objective. The dispute is not just whether ownership of a company is private or public. Rather, the right question to ask is, can capitalist potentates act in larger public interest – something fundamentally against their ilk.

Thus the agitation over privatisation of Air India needs to be viewed in a larger context, and contextualized in terms of the contemporary divide that has been scorching the private sector, that is over the question of mergers and acquisitions.

Just like mergers and acquisitions, privatisation involves the displacement of one set of managers entrusted by shareholders – the citizens – with another set, who may answer to a very different set of shareholders whose only overbearing desire would be to strip Air India of all its value and worth if that helps them to profiteer leaving it as a ghost of a company in the process. This is what the reckless disinvestment of the erstwhile NDA years did to many Public Sector companies between 1999-2004.

What is the gravest charge against Air India - that it is not profitable and it is being crushed under a mountain of debt to the tune of Rs 52,000 crore? The first allegation is untrue. Air India made an operating profit of Rs 105 crore and a net loss after tax of Rs 3,836.77 crore in the 2015-16 fiscal. In the current year, Air India is projected to earn an operating profit of Rs 300 crore and net loss after tax of Rs 3,643 crore.

This is what the junior minister of Civil Aviation Jayant Sinha told the Rajya Sabha in the recently concluded budget session, further adding that there was no proposal to either disinvest or privatise the national carrier.

A profound query then arises - what has changed between the end of March 2017 when the Rajya Sabha was given this written reply and now? What is the deal and with whom?

As has been argued and reiterated by Air India ad-nauseam, the decision to buy new aircraft or merge both Air India and Indian Airlines was of the then UPA government. The fact that it did not work as intended is not the fault of the airline or it's employees and they cannot be penalized for it.

The next argument in favor of privatisation, that the private sector knows how to run Airlines, is also warped. Each time an Air India-type company manages to stay afloat despite efforts of successive governments and managements to run it into the ground, two private airlines have failed in India since the skies were opened in 1992. Few would remember that the first private airline was East-West. It went belly up. What happened to Air Deccan and Damania Airways? Then there is Kingfisher Airlines – the king of good times whose promoter Vijay Mallya ran away with the salary of his own airline employees and is living it up in London.

If privatisation is the panacea for all problems then why doesn't government outsource municipal functions for our cities? Why doesn't the government privatise the Railways, for even the New Delhi railway station is more often than not in a worse condition than a slum?

Why is Air India always picked upon, considering it is still a pot of honey over which hungry vultures have been salivating over two decades now. It has prime real estate across the world, prestigious parking slots at every international airport, bilateral rights, fifth freedom rights in some cases, profitable and even subsidiary companies. The whole package is worth over five lakh crore if properly valued and not the 20,000 odd crores or even much less that the government wants to hawk it off for.

If Prime Minister Modi or his Finance/Defence Minister indeed want to professionalize the Airline and liberate it from the tyranny of the Civil Aviation Ministry they should first write off Air India's debt once and for all. If banks are ready to forgo a substantive part of the 6 lakh crores lent to private companies that have become non performing assets, why is Air India being singled out for step- motherly treatment?

The government should ask financial institutions to pick

up equity in Air India, like private companies have done with the company that owns the Goods and Services Tax Network (GSTN). Third, it should put a specialized board and management in place. Air India can be turned around as a sterling public-private enterprise. You do not need to peddle family silver to some carpetbagger.

The Indian Express
4 July 2017

WHY DEMONETIZATION IS ILLEGAL

On 8 November 2016, the Prime Minister of India announced on television that 86 percent of the money in circulation in the country's economy stood demonetized. With a grand flourish that could have only rivalled a Tughluqi firman (and I can claim copyright to this phrase as I coined it on Twitter to describe this whimsical diktat on the night of 8 November 2016 at 9.07 pm), he announced that his government had scrapped the Rs 500 and Rs 1,000 notes effective from the stroke of the midnight hour.

To put the Tughluqi firman in its historical context, there was a monarch who ruled India from 1324 to 1351 AD. His name was Muhammad bin Tughluq. He was renowned for his whimsical ways. He shifted his capital from Delhi to Devgiri in Maharashtra and renamed it Daultabad. He promptly shifted it back to Delhi when trouble broke out in Bengal and the North-West Frontier Province. Thousands perished as a consequence of this idiosyncratic experiment.

Another quirky try-out was replacing gold coins with copper ones. When famine-like conditions and frequent revolts began straining his coffers, Tughluq found it challenging to sustain the stock of the gold (dinar) and silver (adli) coins on a macro scale. So, he introduced a token currency system and minted vast quantities of new copper and brass coins (tankas) that could be exchanged for fixed amounts of gold and silver.

While this choice helped the Sultanate's finances initially, it also proved profitable for forgers, who began issuing a large number of fake coins. Loopholes such as a simple design (the coins just had some inscriptions) and no royal seals made the task easier for forgers. Every house became a mint for copper coins, while gold and silver coins were zealously hoarded. Soon, the market was awash with fake coins.

As good money was driven out of circulation, the token coins became virtually worthless, leading to hyperinflation. Foreign traders also refused to accept them, paralyzing trade. Realizing that his scheme had failed, Tughluq withdrew the currency in an attempt to stem the economic chaos.

However, this was not the only time in history that demonetization took place. There are other instances that highlight the incredible fragility of the monetary system. In 1735 AD, Nadir Shah devalued his own currency, turning the double-paisa coin into a single-paisa coin, and ordered moneylenders to store no more than 50 mahmoodis (silver coins) in their shops. Unsatisfied with the economic results of this move, he withdrew the order later and even issued new coins, but by then, the devaluation had already made everyday merchandises costlier.

Interestingly, there are two other examples of demonetization, one in the 7th century China (that allowed paper notes to be exchanged for gold, silver, or silk) and one in the 13th century by the Persian king Gaykhatu (whose experiment caused so much chaos that he had to backtrack within eight days).

With that late-evening announcement, Prime Minister Modi found himself in the rather notorious company of the likes of Muhammad bin Tughluq and Nadir Shah.

The prime minister laid out three objectives for demonetization: to curb black money, weed out counterfeit currency, and circumscribe terror financing. Before we examine as to how the government fared on these three fronts that it claimed as the rationale for its foible, let us examine the conceptual legal underpinnings of demonetization.

India has carried out demonetization twice before, once in 1946 and then again in 1978. The first and the second demonetization exercises were executed by ordinances and validated by Acts of Parliament. Section 26(A) of the Reserve Bank of India (RBI) Act 1934 legalized the first demonetization. It reads as follows:

'Notwithstanding anything contained in Section 26, no banknote of the denominational value of five hundred rupees, one thousand rupees or ten thousand rupees issued before the 13th day of January, 1946, shall be legal tender in payment or on account for the amount expressed therein.'

The second demonetization was effected by the Morarji Desai government in 1978. Two BJP veterans, Atal Behari Vajpayee and Lal Krishna Advani, were cabinet ministers in that government. Vajpayee, foreign minister in the Janata government, went on to become the country's prime minister, heading a BJP-led coalition in the late 1990s, and Advani, the information and broadcasting minister in the Morarji cabinet, rose to become Vajpayee's home minister and, at one point, deputy prime minister. The move was carried out through the High Denomination Bank Notes (Demonetization) Ordinance, 1978, that came into effect from 16 January 1978. It was subsequently replaced by the High Denomination Bank Notes Demonetization) Act of 1978.

The reason for this is not difficult to discern. Section 26(2) of the RBI Act, under which the latest edition of demonetizationwas brought about, reads as follows:

'On recommendation of the Central Board the Central Government may, by notification in the Gazette of India, declare that, with effect from such date as may be specified in the notification, any series of banknotes of any denomination shall cease to be legal tender save at such office or agency of the Bank and to such extent as may be specified in the notification.'

In the light of the two experiences in the past, let us now closely examine the 8 November announcement. Data available so far does not shed any light on when the central board of the RBI made the recommendation so sacrosanct in making this decision. Who in the government hierarchy considered it?

Since one of the vaunted objectives of the 8 November 2016 Tughluqi fiat was to block the money flow into the terror outfits, root out counterfeit currency, and flush out alleged black money, was there any inter-ministerial consultation at any level before this crucial decision was made? Another fact that is equally disturbing is that a plain reading of Section 26(2) makes it evident that it empowers the government to demonetize any series of bank notes of a particular denomination and not the entire denomination per se.

P Chidambaram, a former finance minister, explained in a television interview a couple of days after the note-swap was announced that, on 23 January 2014, the RBI had decreed that it would withdraw after the 31 March 2014 all currency notes issued before 2005, including those having higher denominations of Rs 500 and Rs 1,000. In other words, that was the permissible level of withdrawal, as per law, for a series of banknotes and not the scrapping of an entire denomination.

Incidentally, the BJP had opposed this withdrawal with one of its rather caustic spokespersons pontificating:

'The idea is unexplainable as to why this has happened... the measure is strongly anti-poor. The latest gimmick of the finance ministry's demonetization of currency notes before 2005 is basically an attempt to obfuscate the issue of black money that is stashed outside the country. The present government is not in a position to measure the correct quantum of black money, because those who have black money will actually convert it into [the] new currency notes. The sufferers are the *aam aurat and aadmi*; those who are illiterate, who have no access to banking facilities. They will be the ones who will be affected by such diversionary measures. People, who have small savings and no bank accounts... [will see] their life savings... targeted.

The present scheme does nothing to remove black money from circulation.'

Should the current demonetization not be measured against the matrix that the BJP had itself spawned in 2014? In the backdrop of the sturdy argument built by the BJP spokesperson, the current phase of demonetization is entirely illegal.

Let's now move onto the next act of 'illegality'. The RBI Act Section 24(1) reads as follows: 'Subject to the provisions of sub-section(2), banknotes shall be of the denominational values of two rupees, five rupees, ten rupees, twenty rupees, fifty rupees, one hundred rupees, five hundred rupees, one thousand rupees, five thousand rupees and ten thousand rupees or of such other denominational values, not exceeding ten thousand rupees, as the Central Government may, on the recommendation of the Central Board, specify in this behalf.'

The denomination of Rs 2,000 does not get enumerated in this section. There is nothing in the public domain that indicates as to where and when the RBI specified Rs 2,000 as legal tender. It, therefore, can be concluded that without amending Section 24(1) and incorporating the Rs 2,000 denomination in the said section, the act of floating the said note in the market was also unlawful.

Coming to the next act of illegality, one needs to ponder how the arbitrary limits on withdrawal of money was imposed without declaring financial emergency under Article 360 of the Constitution. The 8 November 2016 notification under Section 26(2) issued by the Central Government does not give it the authority to do so. It therefore begs the obvious question as to how the government could subject 124 crore people to the ignominy of standing in serpentine queues and being reduced to beggars for their own money, without a valid notification to that effect under law. What India faces today is the spectre of an undeclared financial emergency.

When it comes to the rights of the citizens, the government has no authority to take away the property of the people without legislation. Under Article 300(A) of the Constitution, every person has a legal right to property. Money that is legal tender is property in the hands of each and every citizen. They use this property to buy goods and services or to transact any other business; therefore, under the circumstances, without adequate legislation, the government cannot take away anybody's money, just as you cannot take away someone's land by executive action. That is why Parliament has enacted the Land Acquisition Act. While land may be immoveable property, currency is moveable.

The excruciating inconvenience to the people apart, there is an uneasy question mark over the legality of the entire exercise undertaken by the government. The assumption that all cash is black money is both facile and conceptually flawed. The Supreme Court had reversed the imposition of President's rule in Arunachal Pradesh setting right a warped decision smacking of scant respect for the democratic tenets. It had done so earlier on spectrum allocation and even the allocation of coal mines. Since the apex court is seized of the matter, it may not be an unreasonable expectation, given past precedents, that the 8 November 2016 notification might be quashed rendering this entire exercise void ab infinito.

Finally, on the three objectives that the government had propounded as the raison d'être for demonetization, the government has come up short. Even six months after the recall of the banknotes, the government failed to furnish a figure as to how much of the scrapped Rs 14,86,000 has come back into the banking system. Was it ostensibly more than the scrapped amount and, if so, this obviously led to the conclusion that there was no blackmoney in the Indian economy! That, as everyone knows, would be completely fallacious, to say the least. What it demonstrated, however, is that the currency-swap or *note-badli* was not the way to unearth black money. This objective also dovetailed into the next objective - weeding out counterfeit currency. If more money than what was scrapped had re-entered the rarefied environs of the banking system, this would lead to the conclusion that either there was no counterfeit currency or those who had it had been successful in swapping it for the genuine legitimate ones by now. Was it not incumbent on the government to share with the citizenry the figures about fake currency unearthed as a consequence of this exercise?

The government's third objective behind demonetization was to sink the terrorist curry boat. Starved of the Indian currency, the terror outfits, it was assumed, would be immobilized to carry out their subversive campaign. This seemed to have been premised on a clear estimate that the government had about the quantum of money being regularly funnelled into terror outfits. This was a clear non-sequitur, for had the government any idea about how much money was flowing into which terrorist entity and from where, questions would have been raised as to the steps the government had taken to check it.

There is no black, white, or grey money. Money is Money. What we have in India are two economies - a formal economy and a non-formal economy. The government should have found a way to merge the non-formal economy into the formal one so everything would become transparent and above-board, with the exchequer getting its due share of taxes and earning from penalties for the errant. Instead, the government made a series of retrograde pronouncements - threatening to imprison people for having foreign bank accounts or the old banknotes in their possession. It succeeded in creating a flight of capital and of entrepreneurs. More than a lakh of businesspersons had turned into expatriates in the United Arab Emirates alone. Quite clearly, they opted for this status to evade harassment by the official agencies. As for the government, the stringent legal measures were the only recourse available to deflect attention of people from its inability to fulfil its rash election promise of bringing back all Indian black money stashed away in foreign bank accounts and depositing it in the bank account of every Indian, each one's share being not less than Rs 15,000.

What the government did in the name of demonetization was both callous and slapdash, betraying insensitivity to the suffering of people. In a democratic polity, people should always be at the centre. However, the government's action demonstrated its scant regard for the people's plight.

More than a hundred died standing in the bank queues. If the government harboured the illusion that a few election victories, that too in state Assembly or civic polls, were a referendum on its whimsical policies, then nothing could be further from the truth.

When the citizens of the republic were made to suffer for no fault of theirs, would it be incorrect to say that this Tughluqi firman was anti-people?

Article courtesy of *Demonetization in the Detail*
Palimpsest, 2017

WHY THE MAHARAJA SHOULD NOT BE SOLD OFF

Sunil Jain, on 10 July 2017, wrote a profound piece in this newspaper on the proposed Air India sell off. He began by asking if Air India was worth Rs 5 lakh crore as I had indicatively valued it in my column for *The Indian Express* or, as some others had suggested, its worth only Re 1?

Before I deal with the valuation question there are certain other questions that the 'morticians' of Air India need to answer. First, what public interest is served by privatising public assets? The global experience of the past 27 years is that it only creates oligarchs and oligarchies.

Second, where is the empirical evidence that the private sector can run a better airline. For every one private airline that has been successful since the skies in India opened up in 1992, two have gone belly up. Even the prima donna of private airlines, Jet Airways, is a not much of an experience to write home about. Let me relate a recent experience. On the morning of 11 July I was accompanying the combined opposition candidate for president, Meira Kumar, to Jaipur for campaign. As the web-check-in had failed, I was standing in the queue to collect my economy-class boarding pass, since that is the only configuration ATRs have. The check-in staff was obtuse, rude and arrogant, in that order. Their behaviour could make any government 'babu' blush with shame.

Third, if public-public partnerships can run utilities successfully across the country, the Delhi Metro Railway Corporation (DMRC) that is jointly owned by the Union government and the Delhi government being a classical example, is the 'sell out' of Air India the only solution to its problems? Why can we not explore other ways like the GSTN (Goods and Service Tax Model Network) model whereby public institutional investors hold 50 per cent of the equity and the remaining 50 per cent is distributed among the general public and employees of Air India? The GSTN equity structure is as follows: Union government 24.5 per cent, state governments 24.5 per cent, HDFC 10 per cent, HDFC Bank 10 per cent, ICICI Bank 10 per cent, NSE Strategic Investment Co 10 per cent and LIC Housing Finance Ltd 11 per cent.

Fourth, if crony capitalists, carpetbaggers and scamsters who are in debt to public sector banks to the tune of Rs 6 lakh crore can routinely have their debts restructured over and over again, why can't the government bite the bullet and retire Air India's debt and give it a fresh start?

Fifth, what is the deal and with whom? What happened between the end of March 2017, when the junior minister for civil aviation informed the Rajya Sabha that there is no move to privatise or disinvest in Air India, and Arun Jaitley's assertion that if private airlines can cater to 86 per cent of the Indian traffic, it can then do 100 per cent too? Why this sudden change of heart? Does the government's left hand not know what the right is doing, or the consummation has already been done in the dark and only the motions of a public marriage ceremony are being gone through? These are the questions that the Parliamentary Standing Committee on Civil Aviation, I hope, asked the government when it met on 12 July – or, of course, these would nonetheless be raised in the appropriate judicial forum.

Now, let's turn to the valuation of Air India which has a number of subsidiary companies. Except for two, all others are in profit, including Air India Express that flies the lucrative Gulf routes. That is why there is a proposal under consideration about the 'good Air India' vs the 'bad Air India' paradigm whereby the profitable aspects of Air India are sold to select cronies and the government just winds up the rest of the company in the name non-profitability and cost optimisation, the euphemism of choice to sack lakhs of employees summarily in the private sector everyday.

Sunil Jain argues that it is difficult to value the prime real estate, landing slots, bilateral rights, fifth freedom rights and, of course, the 'art' that Air India possesses, and therefore, it should be sold at its 'enterprise value' that he has calculated at Rs 14,000 crore. By his recommendation, if the government was to divest 51% and retain 49% to be sold at a later date, then Air India would be hawked off for around Rs 7000 crore. I respectfully disagree.

The real value of Air India lies in its legacy and inheritances. In Mumbai alone, it has the iconic building in Nariman Point, plush flats in Bandra and a sprawling complex encompassing hundreds of acres in Kalina. Forget selling them, even if all this real estate is just redeveloped at current FSI (Floor Space Index) being given by the Government of Maharashtra in conjunction with the NBCC or any other public sector construction company, that would be more than enough to retire Air India's debt. Air India has a sprawling complex in tony Vasant Vihar in Delhi and prime real estate all over the globe.

Coming to parking slots at international airports, some of them are grandfather slots dating back to JRD Tata's time. A large number of them are not being used by Air India. Some of them would sell at a premium of millions of dollars. Then, there are fifth freedom rights that Air India has on some international destinations that it does not exploit and are no longer available. Their value is simply incalculable, and if properly auctioned, the sky is the limit. Coming to the bilaterals, Sunil is right that they belong to the government, and not Air India; but as the national carrier, and if I am properly informed, Air India has the right of first refusal. Private Indian carriers started using these bilateral rights after Air India said that it did not have the capacity to optimise them in full. It can thus be safely said the whole package called Air India is worth Rs 5 lakh crore, if not more.

Then, there is the larger national security argument. As government retains a toehold in the communications industry through BSNL and MTNL, and in the broadcasting space through Doordarshan and AIR, it must have its own airline also.

Air India, in the past, has come to the rescue of millions of stranded Indians from Kuwait in the first Gulf war in 1990, from Iraq in the second Gulf War in 2003, and Yemen during the current conflict and myriad other places where brave men and women of Air India have flown without fear or complaint. When volunteers were called for to fly the relief air-craft to Kandahar to negotiate with, service and bring back passengers of hijacked IC-814, the whole airline volunteered. Catch a private Airline doing it!

It is fashionable to bang Air India. Let us not throw the baby out with the bathwater. The government should find other ways of turning it around. That is why I began The Indian Express piece with the proverb, *'Garib ki joru, sa'ab ki bhabhi.'*

Financial Express
14 July 2017

Floundering Governance

MERA BHASHA HI MERA PRASHASAN HAI

On Friday, the NDA/BJP government completed three years in office. The time has come to evaluate performance on both quantitative and qualitative benchmarks. The four indices are social cohesion, internal security, economic development and international relations.

In the past three years, social cohesion has been the biggest casualty. This is primarily because the current government does not believe in the founding vision of India. In their perceived moment under the sun, they want to recast the liberal and pluralistic idea of India that has held the field for the past 70 years.

The ideological godfather of the current government, Rashtriya Swayamsevak Sangh, always had a bigamous position on India's Partition. While in 1956, RSS supremo MS Golwalkar articulated, 'Our motherland has been partitioned... We have to pledge resolutely not to rest content until we have wiped out this blot,' on 17 August 1965, the Bharatiya Jana Sangh (predecessor of the BJP) even passed a resolution at its meeting in Delhi, which stated, 'India's tradition and nationality has not been against any religion. Modern Islam should also not be an obstacle in the way of unity of Indian nation. Real obstacle is separatist politics. Muslims will integrate themselves with the national life and Akhand Bharat (undivided India) will be a reality – unifying India and Pakistan – once we are able to remove this obstacle (separatist politics).'

Interestingly, the poster boy of Hindutva, Veer Savarkar, had the following to say on the two-nation theory on his election as the president of Hindu Mahasabha. While addressing the 19th session of the Mahasabha in 1937 in Ahmedabad, he declared: 'There are two antagonistic nations living side by side in India. Several infantile politicians commit the serious mistake in supposing that India is already welded into a harmonious nation, or that it could be welded thus for the mere wish to do so... India cannot be assumed today to be a Unitarian and homogenous nation. On the contrary, there are two nations in the main: the Hindus and the Muslims, in India.'

Therein lies the dichotomy wherein the ideologues of the current government believe that if religious Partition could not be implemented in its essence in 1947, that is, India for Hindus and Pakistan for Muslims, it should be done now by transforming India into a majoritarian theocracy. The instruments being used are mass communalism masquerading as nationalism, cow vigilantes being let loose, specially on minorities, creative freedoms being proscribed, freedom of speech and expression being brutally crushed and the demonisation of the other by a hysterical, right-wing co-opted and kept media. However, what the Prime Minister does not realise is that he is skidding on a slippery path whose consequences would be portentous for India.

This ideological agenda is impacting governance generally and the management of internal security specifically. Nothing reflects this better than the absolute mess in Kashmir. The ideologically incongruent alliance between the People's Democratic Party and the BJP has proven to be a disaster. The fall in voting percentages from a high of 65.52 per cent in the Assembly elections in the fall of 2014 to a mere seven per cent turnout in the parliamentary byelection for the Srinagar constituency in the summer of 2017 underscores the deep alienation of the Kashmiri people. The fact that the Election Commission is unable to even conduct the other byelection in Anantnag only serves to accentuate the gravity of the situation.

Similarly, it has been unable to articulate a policy towards left-wing extremism in central India where casualties of the paramilitary forces are mounting on a daily basis. Rather than try to fathom that Maoism is more than just a law and order issue that requires a multi-pronged approach not merely focused upon the use of the state's hard power, the government is trying to deflect attention by targeting academicians who may have a certain worldview, but are defiantly not a part of some hydra-headed reptile whose head lies in the dense jungles of Abujmarh.

Turning to north-eastern India you are confronted with the apparition of the mythical Naga peace accord, later rechristened as the framework agreement, that was supposed to have been 'the' panacea for the longest running insurgency in India. Signed on 3 August 2015, with much fanfare, the accord seems to have vanished into thin air.

Now turning to the economy. Just the set of five numbers from the monthly report put out by the department of finance tells the story. In 2015-16, the rate of GDP growth was 7.9 per cent. It dipped to 7.1 per cent in 2016-17. If you de-horse the statistical jugglery, that is, changing the base year for measuring GDP from 2004-05 to 2011-12, that gives a fictitious bump of two per cent, the effective rate of GDP growth is only 5.1 per cent. The Index of Industrial Production grew at a rate of 2.6 per cent between April and February 2016 as opposed to a mere 0.4 per cent for the corresponding period between April and February 2016-17. Again, the eight core infrastructure sectors registered a growth of only five per cent in March 2017 as opposed to 9.3 per cent in March 2016.

The growth of money supply on a year-on-year basis also tanked from 10 per cent as on 31 March 2016, to 7.3 per cent on 31 March 2017. This is the demonetisation's effect on the Indian economy. And, finally, the dollar that stood at Rs 58.57 on 17 May 2014, climbed by Rs 5.46 and was trading at Rs 64.03 on 17 May 2017.

The net effect of this gross macro economic mismanagement has been that India is now hostage to a spectre of jobless growth. Just one comparative data point illustrates this reality. During the three years, from 2009 to 2011, as India's GDP was galloping at an average 8.5 per cent, notwithstanding the great economic meltdown of 2008, the organised sector was creating, on an average, 9.5 lakh new jobs every year. In the last two years, 2015 and 2016, the average employment generation has dived to less than two lakh jobs a year. This is fewer than 25 per cent of the annual employment generated before 2011.

Now turning to international affairs, the recent One Belt, One Road conference in Beijing exposed India's splendid isolation in the transnational arena. Despite a valid claim that one of the strands of OBOR – the China-Pakistan Economic Corridor – violates India's sovereignty, the government was not able to carry a single neighbouring country with the sole exception of Bhutan, what to talk of world powers.

On Pakistan, the government has tied itself in knots as a consequence of the repeated flip-flops, U-turns and summersaults. It has failed to finesse the power dynamic between US, Russia and China and India's perceived US tilt saw the Russians doing military exercises with Pakistan for the first time in 70 years. There has been no movement on India's permanent membership of either the United Nations Security Council or the Nuclear Suppliers Group in the past three years.

Therein lies the message for the Opposition that 'mera bhashan hi mera prashasan hai' syndrome underscores that even messianic oratory and demagoguery can substitute for governance in our nation.

The Asian Age
27 May 2017

SUPERSESSION: ALL HAVE THE RIGHT TO ASK QUESTIONS

As the newsbreak flashed across television screens last Saturday evening, 17 December that the Indian Army and the Air Force would have new Chiefs, Lt Gen. Bipin Rawat and Air Marshal BS Dhanoa respectively, I immediately tweeted asking the Prime Minister as to why two or, perhaps, even three officers senior to Gen. Rawat, had been superseded by his government. Even a week later, there are no answers forthcoming from the government, much less the prime minister. For quite some time, the social media, strategic community, veterans' WhatsApp groups and even the 'langargup (mess gossip)' within the services was abuzz with speculation over the impending supersession. In the Army's case, the rumour that came true was that Gen. Rawat would be elevated to the chief over the heads of the Eastern Army Commander Lt Gen. Pravin Bakshi, Southern Army Commander Lt. Gen. Pattiarimal Mohamed Ali Hariz, and Central Army Commander Lt Gen. BS Negi, who ostensibly became an Army commander before Gen. Rawat.

The first question is: Was this 'deep selection' or supersession necessary? Whenever it has happened in the past, it has left the institution deeply wounded. In 1957, Gen. KS Thimayya was selected over two senior lieutenant-generals - Sant Singh and Kulwant Singh. While the former put in his papers, the latter stayed on. Again in 1983, Gen. Arun Kumar Vaidya was promoted over Lt Gen. SK Sinha, who promptly put in his papers. After that, for a good 33 years, the seniority principle held the field and perhaps for good reason. Without casting even a whisper of an insinuation on the professionalism or the brilliance of Lt Gen. Rawat as either a commander or a solider, the source-based reasoning that has been put out by the government for its action has not been accepted by retired service officers.

Lt Gen. Ike Singha (Retd) put out a Facebook post entitled 'Surgical strike on the Indian Army,' where he critiqued the rationale of the government. It may be pertinent to point out that Gen. Singha was head of the peacekeeping mission in Golan Heights in Syria and Israel from 2012 to 2015. Similarly, Lt Gen. Harwant Singh, the former deputy chief of Army Staff, concluded a piece in a national daily with the following lines: 'In the present case, the government has simply failed to come up with any compelling reasons to break the chain of seniority and has, in fact, politicized the appointment of the Army Chief.' In a tweet, Lt Gen. Tej Sapru put it as follows: 'Violation of norms of seniority by the govt. in selection of COAS, a sad day for the armed forces. Not good for the system'. Lt Gen. Panag in a piece concludes with the following advice to the government: 'Last but not the least, to partially undo the damage done to the Indian Army, the government should make use of the two eminent, superseded generals either in the proposed higher defence management structure or at any other appropriate level. It would be unfair to make them serve under a junior. Their loss of honour because of an ambiguous selection process, if not restored, will have an adverse effect on the morale of the Indian Army.'

However, the profoundest rationale for not bypassing the seniority principle came from the former Vice-Chief of the Army, Lt Gen. Vijay Oberoi. In an article, he wrote: 'I need to narrate a discussion held on the sidelines of a seminar at the College of Defence Management Secunderabad, many years back. During a discussion I had with two cerebral military intellectuals - Gen. Raghavan and Air Vice Marshal Kak - the three of us discussed the pros and cons of selecting a service chief on the basis of seniority, as was the norm vis-à-vis an open-ended selection from the C's-in-C. After weighing the issue with great deliberation, we came to the conclusion that there were more negatives in the latter, as chances of selection based on political, sycophantic and non-professional reasons may become predominant in due course, with professional and character qualities being sacrificed on account of extraneous issues. With such precedence, even appointments of Army and corps commanders may meet such a fate later, throwing professionalism to the winds.'

It is, therefore, apparent that the logic of deep selection has not cut any ice with the retired top brass of the armed forces, though it may be only fair to point out that some retired officials have also supported the selection/supersession. These are all grizzled military men, and not some politicos tilting at windmills. That brings us to the second question that the government and the BJP have been harping about and that is: Are political parties entitled to ask questions if the selection processes in the armed forces are a tad strange, if not irregular. This question becomes all the more germane because the government has been trying to run this gauntlet for a while that it is anti-national to question the BJP, seditious to question the government and, in fact, treasonous to even ask legitimate questions of the defence establishment, whether they pertain to operations along the LoC or senior appointments in the three services.

This argument is not only insidious but also ludicrous, to say the least. In all democracies around the world, the principle of civilian supremacy in civil-military relations is well established, if not cast in stone. While the civilian leadership defers or should defer to the armed forces on operational imperatives, the broader trajectory of higher defence management is something that falls squarely to the remit of the civilian leadership. The strategic philosophy that should guide the defence leadership depends on a host of geo-political and geo-economic imperatives as well as relationships or the lack of it with other countries. In furtherance of this dictum, even Parliament has both standing and consultative committees that exercise oversight on the functioning of the defence establishment that is not limited to policy and budgetary matters. It is, therefore, imperative that both parliamentarians and political parties must ask the hard questions when required on matters that impinge on national security.

The Asian Age
24 December 2016

FROM DEPRESSING 2016 TO SCHIZOPHRENIC 2017

'Those who cannot remember the past are condemned to repeat it,' thus spake George Santayana philosopher, essayist, poet and novelist. As we gaze into the crystal ball, read the tea leaves, shuffle the tarot cards, dust the ancient astrological charts trying to find the polestar of 2017, perhaps the best template would be to look back at 2016 - given that India's two fundamental challenges remain Pakistani terror and the perilous state of the Indian economy. Both are symbiotically intertwined.

The previous year started badly with an attack on an Air Force base in Pathankot, coming as it did one week after the Prime Minister of India made an unscheduled stopover in Lahore to wish Nawaz Sharif on his birthday. The deep state in Pakistan did not want to be on the same page as the civilian government.

As someone who was extremely critical of the prime minister's Kabul-Lahore-New Delhi itinerary for a variety of reasons, it must be said in retrospect that Narendra Modi made an audacious and a bold move, perhaps with the right intent but one that was destined to fail.

Unlike President Ashraf Ghani, who tried to stoop to conquer by going to the General Headquarters (GHQ) in Rawalpindi to call on Pakistani Army Chief Gen. Raheel Sharif in November 2014, no Indian prime minister can ever dream of calling on an army chief of any nation, much less Pakistan, even if the Pakistani civilian government would facilitate and encourage such an interaction. It could be another matter if the Pakistan Army Chief came calling on the Indian prime minister either in Islamabad or New Delhi.

That anyway seems to be a surreal fantasy, given that Gen. Pervez Musharraf refused to receive Prime Minister Atal Behari Vajpayee when he travelled to Lahore in March 1998 and, if reports are to be believed, the Pakistan military even refused to accord a guard of honour to Mr Modi when he landed in Lahore on Christmas day in 2015.

Therein lies the conundrum - till the GHQ is not on board there can never be peace in the region. The relationship with Pakistan, therefore, would continue to be in a free-fall for the foreseeable future, at least through the next year.

Nine months later, another attack by uniform-less state actors from Pakistan at an army camp in Uri in Jammu and Kashmir invited retaliation from the Indian side in the form of 'surgical strikes'. Stripped of diplomatic gibberish, what it meant was that the Narendra Modi government had effected a paradigm shift in response to cross-border terror.

This was not the first time border action teams had gone across and annihilated Pakistani border posts or ostensible terrorist launchpads, but what was a first was the public ownership of such actions. This cross-border, publicly owned-up action by the BJP-NDA government left a number of questions unanswered. If this was intended to bring about a behavioural change in the Pakistani establishment, clearly that does not seem to have happened. Though there have not been other attacks as lethal as the one in Uri in the past four months, there has been no let-up in the efforts by the proxies of Pakistan.

From a strategic perspective, has the government now taken a decision that a conventional tactical response would be the sine qua non to any major terrorist outrage emanating from Pakistan? If that is the case, then we may be looking at an escalatory spiral in 2017 for the Pakistani deep state is sure to test out this new threshold. An armed conflict with Pakistan, the nature and intensity of which may be hard to predict, in

2017 should not be treated as strictly off the table. It is thus clear that India's albatross around the neck and its Achilles heel are both hyper-engaged.

Let's turn to the domestic front, and Mr Modi's demonetization move on 8 November 2016. How the three objectives put forth - unearthing black money, exorcising counterfeit currency and circumscribing terrorist financing - can be achieved by a currency swap defies imagination.

The fact that Mr Modi was able to carry off the greatest pain that has been caused to every single individual since the Partition of India should be a cause for reflection for the Opposition. Why did the people of India not rise up like the populace of Venezuela, especially when the trench between the illusion that the prime minister has been trying to create and the reality is so wide?

There are two apposite storylines that have run through human civilization since times immemorial - the inclusive chronicle, which anchors the liberal, democratic construct, and the stentorian patriarch, who believes in the dictum 'spare the rod and spoil the child'. Mr Modi has been pushing the latter narrative for the past 30-odd months - the strict father who administers bitter medicine to his children and coerces them to believe it is for their own good.

After 10 years of a soft-touch UPA rule, where the government had a very benign presence and everybody had a virtual free run in terms of experimenting with innovative forms of creativity, grotesque varieties of criticism, and unsubstantiated forms of calumny, it almost seems as if the nation is thrusting for the whiplashes that Mr Modi is administering.

Extrapolated over the year ahead, it means that Mr Modi would be emboldened to take more rash and whimsical decisions, to say the least. As the pressure on the economy grows as a consequence of the implications of demonetization playing out, one can surely expect more strikes of the Tughluqi variety on bank lockers and even legitimately acquired property.

The failure of the political Opposition to organize any street protests of any significance, let alone the television spectacles that were witnessed in 2011, would ensure that the totalitarian, despotic, and populist attempt to morph from a corporate clone to a babbling socialist tilting at the windmills, a rib-tickling version of Che Guevara, would only exacerbate. 2016 was just a baby step in trying to anchor the discourse 90 degrees to the right. This year will see this come to fruition with the flower of divisiveness in full bloom. If 2016 was depressing, 2017 could be schizophrenic.

The Asian Age
7 January 2017